ATTITUDE TOWARDS MIGRATION AMONG RURAL RESIDENTS: STAGES AND FACTORS INVOLVED IN THE DECISION TO MIGRATE

BY: SAMIR N. MAAMARY

San Francisco, California

1976

Published in 1976 by

R AND E RESEARCH ASSOCIATES
4843 Mission Street, San Francisco 94112
18581 McFarland Avenue, Saratoga, California 95070

Publishers and Distributors of Ethnic Studies
Adam S. Eterovich
Robert D. Reed

Library of Congress Card Catalog Number

75-36559

ISBN

0-88247-402-2

ACKNOWLEDGEMENTS

I am greatly indebted to Dr. C. Milton Coughenour, my advisor and the chairman of my Ph.D. committee, for his close supervision and continuous guidance throughout my graduate studies and formulating and writing of this dissertation. His moral support and readiness and willingness to help beyond the call of duty were extremely helpful to me during trying periods.

My sincere appreciation is also extended to all the members of my special committee: Drs. Walter F. Abbott, John Stephenson, James S. Brown, and Jan Luytjes. This dissertation reflects their useful comments and many valuable contributions.

I am specially grateful for Drs. Rabel J. Burdge and Eldon D. Smith, who at the last days have been kind enough to accept serving on my committee, replacing Drs. James S. Brown and Jan Luytjes.

To the East Tennessee Development District and its executive director, John W. Anderson, Jr., I am very grateful for their cooperation throughout the study and their permission for the use of the data.

A special word of appreciation is extended to my wife, Rosie, for her countless hours of typing and her moral support throughout my graduate studies and writing this dissertation; I am most grateful.

To my daughter, Barbara Sophia, who, at moments of high pressure, did not receive Daddy's full attention and sometimes was unjustifiably scolded or put to bed, I extend my apologies.

Finally, I would like to express my appreciation to Mrs. Linda Holt for her services and fine work in typing this dissertation, to the Department of Sociology, University of Kentucky, and to Mrs. Cornelia Morgan for their cooperation and assistance in the use of the computing center.

TABLE OF CONTENTS

LIST OF TABLES

LIST OF FIGURES

CHAPTER I

INTRODUCTION

Very few social phenomena have been attended to by as many academic disciplines or investigated by as many social scientists as has migration. The number of research studies conducted by demographers, economists, sociologists, psychologists, human geographers, political scientists, and statisticians is in the thousands. Interest in the field of migration is not accidental, for it touches many aspects of man's life: fertility, mortality, population composition, economic growth, social change, social problems, social adjustment, to name a few.

The importance of migration as a phenomenon, when assessed in terms of number of people that move, its impact on people, on sending and receiving communities, and on the nation as a whole, can hardly be over-emphasized. In the United States, for example, approximately one-fifth of the civilian population one year old and over move annually. Five percent of heads of families move each year between labor markets. Fifty-seven percent of all heads of families are not living where they were when they left school.[1] And judging from past trends, the rate of migration is likely to rise in the future as population growth, modernization, and improvement in the means of communication and transportation continue to take place.

The reasons for, or causes of, migration are varied and complex, and so are the consequences of migration. Some view migration as an adaptive process, others see it as socially disruptive. But regardless of the reasons for moving and whether migration is constructive or disruptive, people continue to move in great numbers each year within and between nations.

Most of past migration studies centered on the effects of migration, reasons for moving, direction of migration, characteristics of migrants, characteristics of sending and receiving areas, and obstacles to mobility. A host of economic, social, psychological, cultural, and situational factors in migration have been investigated. Yet, regardless of the substantial volume of research studies on the subject, the diverse disciplines dealing with it, and the many factors related to it, a review of the literature reveals that migration phenomena are still little understood, poorly conceptualized, and lack adequate theoretical orientation. The majority of migration studies, internal and international, have tended to be discrete, descriptive, and with little or no attention to a theoretical framework as a basis for a research orientation or for the formulation of conclusions. As Mangalam rightly remarks, "Theoretical statements that do exist in the contemporary literature, while useful and adequate for interpreting a specific segment of the migration field or for making sense out of specific data in each instance, largely fail to provide a general framework within which the vast amount of existing facts from different migration studies can be integrated and given meaning."[2]

Lack of generalized theories of migration is related to the low abstraction and poor conceptualization of the migration phenomenon.[3] The inadequacy in abstraction and conceptualization contributes to inadequate model-building, inquiry, analysis and manipulation of variables, and, in many cases, to faulty inferences. This, in turn, contributes to incomplete explanation of the migration process. Commenting on this subject, Mangalam and Schwarzweller state that "most of the migration studies reported in the recent literature reveal, in our judgment, serious inadequacies in the manner that migration, as a phenomenon, is abstracted. This, in turn, leads to misconception about the nature of migration and, hence, to definitional difficulties, segmentalized research activity (i.e., narrow and highly discipline-bound), and a fragmented theoretical development."[4]

Research Objective

The need for a general theoretical framework that can organize and interpret migration data of diverse kinds and weld them into an integrated and meaningful explanatory system has been stressed by many scholars.[5] Very little has been added to the theoretical guidelines and assumptions set forth decades ago by E. G. Ravenstein's "Laws of Migration," Dorothy S. Thomas' "Push-Pull Hypothesis," Samuel A. Stouffer's "Theory of Intervening Opportunities," and Zipf's "P_1P_2/D Hypothesis," in spite of the mounting evidence contradicting the adequacy and validity of these theories.

A general integrated theory will not only serve to organize and interpret existing data, but will also help in orienting new research studies in a more systematic and fruitful manner. While it is highly desirable to build a general theoretical framework of migration, the task will not be easy considering the extensive body of data about the subject and the many disciplines and factors involved. Difficult as the task may be, it is not insurmountable and, unless this is done, the migration field will not merit the appellation of science.

The basic objective of this study is to determine the factors underlying different stages in the decision-making process of voluntary
migration, and the relationship of these factors to one another and to
migration.

Migration is viewed as a process composed of three stages: deprivation, predisposition to move, and migration.[6] Each stage is a
necessary but not sufficient condition for the stage following it. The
significance of different factors will be evaluated in relation to migration at each stage.

Plan of the Research

To accomplish the above objectives, the study will proceed in three
stages:

1. Review and evaluation of current stage of migration theories
and research. This is dealt with in Chapter II.

2. Integrate relevant facts into a meaningful and comprehensive
theoretical framework, showing the various factors involved and their
relationships to one another and to the various stages of the migration
process, which is the concern of Chapter III.

3. Test the basic assumptions of the model with data from a random
sample of rural population in Tennessee. This is discussed in Chapter V.

Chapter IV presents the methodology including the measurement of
concepts, hypotheses, population studied, data collection, and research
design. Suggestions and recommendations for further research are discussed in Chapter VI.

Footnotes

1. U.S. Department of Commerce, Bureau of the Census, Current Popula-
   tion Reports, Population Characteristics Series, p. 20; John B.
   Lansing and Eva Mueller, The Geographic Mobility of Labor (Ann
   Arbor, Michigan: 1967), p. 335.

2. J. J. Mangalam, Human Migration: A Guide to Migration Literature
   in English 1955-1962 (Lexington, 1968), p. 1.

3. For example, very few students have dealt with the process of
   migration, and none has dealt with it adequately or completely,
   not to mention having tested it.

4. J. J. Mangalam and Harry K. Schwarzweller, "General Theory in the Study of Migration: Current Needs and Difficulties," _The International Migration Review_, III (Fall, 1968), pp. 10-11. Mangalam and Schwarzweller differentiate between abstraction and conceptualization in that the first implies 'originating observations' while the latter refers to 'translating this original imagery to communicate words in the form of a workable definition.'

5. See, for example, Mangalam and Schwarzweller, op. cit., pp. 3-18; Rupert B. Vance, "Is Theory for Demographers?" _Population Theory and Policy_, eds., Joseph J. Spengler and Otis Dudley Duncan (Glencoe, Illinois, 1956), pp. 88-94; John R. Folger, "Models in Migration," _Selected Studies of Migration Since World War II_, Proceedings of the 34th Annual Conference of the Milbank Memorial Fund, 1957, pp. 155-164; William Petersen, _Population_ (New York, 1961), pp. 592-621; Everett S. Lee, "A Theory of Migration," _Demography_, III (1966), pp. 47-57.

6. Due to limitations of data, plans to move rather than the act of migration itself will be used in this study as the major dependent variable.

CHAPTER II

A REVIEW OF THEORY AND RESEARCH ON MIGRATION

Theory

Generalizations about migration have been advanced by several population specialists under various headings: laws of migration, theories of migration, models of migration, and typology and hypotheses of migration. The ones often used or quoted in the migration literature will be reviewed. Criticism of these theories, models, etc., will be left until the end of this chapter.

A. Ravenstein's Laws of Migration

One of the earliest and most noted theorists on migration is E. G. Ravenstein from England. On March 17, 1885, at the Royal Statistical Society, Ravenstein presented his famous paper on "The Laws of Migration."[1] This paper was based upon the British Census of 1881. Ravenstein's paper was highly criticized by many of his colleagues. However, the criticism of his colleagues did not diminish his conviction that these laws were valid nor deter his effort to prove it. In 1889, he bolstered his views with data from more than twenty countries. This second paper was also entitled "The Laws of Migration."[2] Ravenstein's laws as outlined and explained in his two papers are summarized below:

1. _The economic factor and employment opportunities predominate other factors_: Bad or oppressive laws, heavy taxation, an attractive climate, uncongenial social surroundings, and even compulsion (slave trade, transportation), all have produced and are still producing currents of migration, but none of these currents can compare in volume with that which arises from the desire inherent in most men to 'better' themselves in material respects. It is thus that the surplus population of one part of the country drifts into another part, where the development of procuring productive land still in a state of nature, calls for more hands to labour.[3]

2. _Migrants travel short distances_: We have already proved that the great body of our migrants only proceed a short

distance, and that there takes place consequently a uni-
versal shifting or displacement of the population, which
produces 'currents of migration' setting in the direction
of the great centers of commerce and industry which
absorb the migrants.

Migrants enumerated in a certain centre of absorption will
consequently grow less with the distance proportionately
to the native population which furnishes them.[4]

In his second paper, Ravenstein elaborates further on the relationship between migration and distance. He states:

Suppose there exists a surplus of labour in one province
and a deficiency in another, whilst the intervening provinces are able to find remunerative occupation for all
their inhabitants. Will the labourer, in search of work,
travel across these intervening provinces, in order to
supply the deficiency? I say, no! The want will be sup-
plied from the immediate neighborhood, and its effect
will travel from province to province until it makes itself felt in the most remote among them.[5]

The inhabitants of the country immediately surrounding a
town of rapid growth flock into it; the gaps thus left in
the rural population are filled up by migrants from more
remote districts, until the attractive force of one of
our rapidly growing cities makes its influence felt, step
by step, to the most remote corner of the kingdom.[6]

3. Large industrial cities induce long distance migration:
   "Migrants proceeding long distances generally go by preference to one of the great centers of commerce and industry."[7]

4. Current and counter-current: "...each main current produces a counter-current of feebler strength."[8]

5. Rural-urban migration differential: "The natives of town
   are less migratory than those of the rural parts of the
   country."[9]

6. "Females are more migratory than males."[10]

7. Migration increases as technology and industrialization
   take place: "Does migration increase? I believe so!...
   Whenever I was able to make a comparison I found that an
   increase in the means of locomotion and a development of
   manufactures and commerce have led to an increase of migration."[11]

B. Socioeconomic Push-Pull Theory

The socioeconomic push-pull theory, which is often called the "push-pull hypothesis," is the most used theory, explicitly or implicitly, by population researchers in explaining and predicting migration. According to this theory, migration results from socioeconomic imbalances between communities, regions, or countries; certain factors "pushing" persons away from the area of origin, and other factors "pulling" them to the area of destination. Push factors refer to dissatisfaction with local conditions prior to a move, and pull factors refer to the awareness of advantageous conditions elsewhere, i.e., an attractive force. It is generally hypothesized that migration tends to proceed from less to more "prosperous" areas.[12]

C. Zipf's P_1P_2/D Hypothesis

This hypothesis was introduced by George K. Zipf in 1945. It relates migration to distance and population size. Three basic assumptions underly this hypothesis. They are:

1. The rate of in-migration to a central point from each of several other points lying at a distance tends to vary inversely with the distance.[13]

2. The rate of out-migration from a central point to each of several points lying at a distance tends to vary inversely with distance.[14]

3. The amount of interchange between any two areas is directly proportional to the product of the population of the two areas and inversely proportional to the distance between them.[15]

D. Theory of Intervening Opportunities

The theory of intervening opportunities was introduced by Samuel A. Stouffer in 1940. In a sense it integrates three theories: Ravenstein's "laws" on migration and distance, Zipf's P_1P_2/D hypothesis, and theory of competing migrants. This theory assumes that the number of persons going a given distance is directly proportional to the percentage increase in opportunities at that distance, and that there is no necessary relationship between mobility and distance. Instead, it introduces the concept of "intervening opportunities." It proposes that "the number of persons going a given distance is directly proportional to the number of opportunities at that distance and inversely proportional to the number of intervening opportunities."[16] Opportunities were left undefined, but were operationally measured in terms of houses and apartment vacancies.[17]

7

E.   Theory of Labor Markets

The theory of labor markets or spatial mobility of labor is most adhered to by economists. It assumes that the volume of movement of the labor force is determined by the number of jobs available at destination, regardless of the characteristics of: (a) the people, (b) the place of residence, or (c) the place of destination. Given differential availability of jobs between two areas, the adherent of this view would expect the movement to take place from the area of less to the area of more jobs. Who moves, according to this view, is a separate and essentially secondary question.[18]

F.   Lee's Multifactor Theory

In an attempt to develop a theory of migration, Everett S. Lee conceptualized migration as involving a set of factors at origin and destination, a set of intervening obstacles, and a series of personal factors. Then from this model he formulated a series of hypotheses about the volume of migration under varying conditions, the development of stream and counter-stream, and the characteristics of migrants. The hypotheses are summarized below:

On Volume of Migration

1. "The volume of migration within a given territory varies (directly) with the degree of diversity of areas included in that territory."[19]

2. "The volume of migration varies (directly) with the diversity of people."[20]

3. "The volume of migration varies inversely with the difficulty of surmounting the intervening obstacles."[21]

4. "The volume of migration increases during periods of economic expansion, and decreases during depressions."[22]

5. "Unless severe checks are imposed, both the volume and rate of migration tend to increase with time."[23]

6. "The volume and rate of migration vary with the state of progress in a country and area."[24]

On Stream and Counterstream

1. "Migration tends to take place largely within well-defined streams."[25]

2. "For every major migration stream, a counterstream develops."[26]

3. "The efficiency of stream (ratio of stream to counterstream or the net redistribution of population effected by the opposite flows) is high if the major factors in the development of migration streams were minus (push) factors at origin."[27]

4. "The efficiency of stream and counterstream tends to be low if origin and destination are similar."[28]

5. "The efficiency of migration streams will be high if the intervening obstacles are great."[29]

6. "The efficiency of migration streams varies with economic conditions, being high in prosperous times and low in times of depression."[30]

On Characteristics of Migrants

1. "Migration is selective..., migrants are not a random sample of the population at origin."[31]

2. "Migrants responding primarily to plus (pull) factors at destination tend to be positively selected (of high quality)."[32]

3. "Migrants responding primarily to minus factors at origin tend to be negatively selected (of low quality)."[33]

4. "Taking all migrants together, selection tends to be bimodal forming a U-shaped curve along poor to excellent continuum."[34]

5. "The degree of positive selection increases with the difficulty of the intervening obstacles."[35]

6. "The heightened propensity to migrate at certain stages of the life cycle is important in the selection of migrants."[36]

7. "The characteristics of migrants tend to be intermediate between the characteristics of the population at origin and the population at destination."[37]

G. Bogue's Generalizations

In discussing migration streams, Donald J. Bogue mentioned that empirical research has supported the validity of twelve generalizations.[38] They are:

1. "The rate of in-migration to a central point from each of several other points lying at a distance tends to vary inversely with the distance."[39]

2. "The rate of out-migration from a central point to each of several other central points lying at a distance tends to vary inversely with the distance."[40]

3. "The amount of interchange between any two areas is directly proportional to the product of the population of the two areas and inversely proportional to the distance between them."[41]

4. "Rates of net migration between two areas tend to be directly proportional to differences in level of living and inversely proportional to the distance between them."[42]

5. "If two areas are in different economic regions, the relationship between distance and number of migrants may be different from the relationship within an economically integrated area."[43]

6. "The number of persons going a given distance is directly proportional to the number of opportunities at that distance and inversely proportional to the number of intervening opportunities."[44]

7. "The rate of migration between two communities varies with the type of community of origin and destination, the direction of migration, and the age and other characteristics of the migrant."[45]

8. "The rate of in-migration and out-migration in any community tend not to be independent of each other. A high rate of in-migration tends to be accompanied by a high rate of out-migration."[46]

9. "A very high proportion of all migration streams is a flow between communities of the same type (urban to urban, farm to farm, etc.). In modern industrialized nations the urban-to-urban flow may be larger than all other flows combined."[47]

10. "Migration streams tend to avoid areas of high unemployment and to flow with greatest velocity toward areas of low unemployment."[48]

11. "The size, direction, and net effect of migration streams are not invariable, either in time or in place. Instead, they are highly sensitive to the social and economic changes that are occurring in the various communities of origin and destination."[49]

12. "The regional pattern of net migration tends to remain constant for several decades, presumably reflecting the continued action of a given set of redistributive forces."[50]

H. Petersen's Typological Theory

Noting the inadequacy of migration "theories" and "laws" in general, Petersen states: "...we cannot formulate valid 'laws,' for the empirical regularities do not always hold. The ultimate generalization in this case is a typology, in which the various conditions under which migration takes place are related to its probable effects."[51] Then Petersen took the push-pull theory as a guiding framework for his typology, and after refining it by distinguishing innovating from conservative migration and by including in the analysis the migrants' level of aspiration that the push-pull theory lacked, Petersen arrived at five broad classes of migration: primitive, forced, impelled, free, and mass migration.[52] A summary of the general typology of migration formed by Petersen and various factors and interactions involved are shown in Table 1.

Evaluation and Criticism of Migration Theories

In brief, the above generalizations relate migration to opportunities at areas of residence and destination, characteristics of sending and receiving communities, characteristics of migrants, and distance between sending and receiving communities. Many of these generalizations overlap and sometimes compete and contradict one another. Furthermore, while each one of them emphasizes one aspect or a limited number of factors, none of the theories or sets of hypotheses covers the entire migration process.

The terms "laws" and "theories" used to describe these assumptions are inappropriate. None qualifies as a theory, much less a law in the fullest sense. For a theory should explain more adequately and fully all or any aspect of the migration phenomenon. A law, on the other hand, needs much more testing before it can be reasonably established. This is far from being the case of the above generalizations. Descriptive or "absolute" hypothesis is the most appropriate term to describe these statements.[53] All fail to specify the causal factors and the necessary and sufficient conditions under which migration will take place. Consequently, these hypotheses, like all descriptive hypotheses, never establish cause-effect relationships, nor do they explain adequately the migration phenomenon.

Deficiencies of each major generalization are further examined below.

A. Socioeconomic Push-Pull Theory

As noted earlier, the push-pull theory explains that migration is due to socioeconomic imbalances between regions, certain factors "pushing" persons away from the area of origin, and others "pulling" them to the area of destination. Push factors refer to dissatisfactions with local condi-

TABLE 1

GENERAL TYPOLOGY OF MIGRATION[54]

Type of Interaction	Migratory Force	Class of Migration	Type of Migration	
			Conservative	Innovating
Nature and man	Ecological push	Primitive	Wandering Ranging	Flight from the land
State (or equivalent) and man	Migration policy	Impelled	Flight	Coolie trade
		Forced	Displacement	Slave trade
Man and his norms	Higher aspirations	Free	Group	Pioneer
Collective behavior	Social momentum	Mass	Settlement	Urbanization

tions prior to move, and pull factors refer to awareness of advantageous conditions elsewhere.

The main limitations of this theory are that it is expressed in such vague and broad terms that it does not actually explain anything. For example, it does not specify what these pull and push factors are, and consequently it cannot be verified. Furthermore, the push-pull theory does not provide for the interaction between the pull and push factors that most often act simultaneously on people's decision to migrate. For example, it does not explain what would happen if the push and pull factors work in the opposite directions - strong push factors and weak pull factors or weak push factors and strong pull factors.

Another major shortcoming of the push-pull theory is its failure to take into account the effects of confounding factors such as personal characteristics and attitudes - age, education, aspiration, etc. - feasibility of opportunities, distance involved, cost of move, etc. For not all people respond to push and pull factors equally nor can everyone make the move, even if he wants to do so.

In brief, the push-pull theory is a partial theory stated in unconditional terms.

B. Theory of Intervening Opportunities

No attempt will be made here to evaluate or dispute the neatness and accuracy of the mathematical formula of the theory of intervening opportunities advanced by Stouffer. For regardless of the validity of the formula, the theory is simply descriptive and does not tell us anything about the causes of migration nor the various factors related to migration other than destination opportunities and intervening opportunities. Furthermore, opportunities and intervening opportunities were defined as the sum of migrants, which takes as a premise the thing that must be explained. And suppose that opportunities and intervening opportunities become defined, the theory will continue to be inadequate to completely explain the migration phenomenon. It explains only half as much as the push-pull theory does, for the theory accounts for only the factors (opportunities) in area of destination, and ignores completely the factors in the area of residence as well as the characteristics of migrants, all of which affect migration.

C. Theory of Labor Markets

Although no one would deny the importance of the economic factor, it is inaccurate to attribute all movement of people to the quest for economic gain as assumed by the theory of labor market. Some moves are made for family reasons, health reasons, educational reasons, or community reasons. Most moves are made, not for one single reason but for a combination of reasons. Thus the economic determinism of the theory of labor market is only a partial explanation of the causes of the migration phenomenon. Furthermore, the theory fails to take into account many of the intervening and conditional factors: competing opportunities in other places, characteristics of migrants, characteristics of area of destination, and distance, all of which may limit or facilitate actual migration.

D. Zipf's P_1P_2/D Hypothesis

This hypothesis is more a predictive proposition than a causal theory. It simply relates distance to mobility, that is, migration is inversely related to distance. All other factors are ignored. It is an adequate hypothesis in its own right, in that it predicts the migration stream between various areas based on distance and population. However, it fails to explain the reasons for which people migrate, whether this be a short or long distance, for people move for better opportunities and not just for shorter distances. This point is well explained by the theory of intervening opportunities.

Regarding E. Ravenstein's laws of migration, Lee's theoretical assumptions, and Bogue's generalizations, they are partial macro theories or hypotheses that consider only one factor at a time at the group level. As such, they offer partial and simplistic explanations of human behavior and the migration phenomenon. Furthermore, as will be shown later in the review of research studies, each of these hypotheses, except probably for age and education, has been disproved by some studies.

Research

In very few areas of sociology can the number and diversity of research studies match those on migration. Research studies in more than a half dozen academic disciplines have been conducted to determine factors influencing variation in mobility. Among the major factors that have been investigated are: socioeconomic conditions at the area of residence; socioeconomic conditions at the area of destination; types of sending and receiving communities; means of communication and transportation; distance; characteristics of migrants such as age, aspiration, intelligence, education, income, occupational skills, sex, social class, race, marital status, family and community ties, family size, family structure, parents' occupation, employment status, past moves, etc.; and reasons for moving. Each factor has been investigated many times. The result is a lack of agreement regarding the level of significance, the strength, and direction of relationship between migration and each of these factors. This lack of agreement among research findings has led several population researchers to conclude that migration is random and no generalizations could be made. In reviewing the literature on migration selectivity, Bogue notes that: "Almost all of the migration differentials that one cares to state can be shown to have important exceptions." Then Bogue goes on and outlines six differentials that he believes are valid at the present time. They are:

"(1) Persons in late teens, twenties, and early thirties are much more mobile than younger or older persons...(2) Men tend to be more migratory than women, especially over long distances and when the conditions at the destination are insecure or difficult. (3) The rate of migration from an area tends to vary inversely with the general level of educational attainment in that area. (4) Persons with professional occupations are among the most migratory segments of the population, while laborers and operatives are much below average in the degree of their mobility. (5) Unemployed persons are more migratory than employed persons. (6) Negroes are less migratory than white persons."[55]

Edmund de S. Brunner, after reviewing research studies about rural migration, states that findings emerging from practically all studies of migration and population mobility show that:

(1) Females leave rural areas, especially farms, in dispro-portionately larger numbers and at an earlier age than males. (2) The bulk of the rural-urban migration begins at age 16 and is over by age 30. (3) While a majority of migrating youth in their first move settle near their parents' homes, the better educated go further. (4) The greater the dis-tance a migrant moves, the more likely it is that his desti-nation is a large city. (5) The youth of tenant familes are more mobile than those of owner families, but they move shorter distances. (6) Males, though less migratory than females, travel farther. (7) Nearby cities attract dispro-portionately large proportions of unskilled workers from rural America, more distant and larger cities a higher pro-portion of more capable and professional workers. (8) Younger families are more mobile than older, operators of small farms than those with larger holdings. (9) Families with a number of organizational contacts in their community are less mobile than those with few. (10) Rates of migra-tion tend to vary with urban economic conditions.[56]

The above statements are by no means universally valid. Contradic-tory results are occasionally found. A sample of some of the findings of research studies on migration is presented below. The factors investi-gated will be classified under four general categories: reasons for moving, characteristics of migrants, characteristics of sending and receiving communities, and others.

A. Reasons for Moving

People's reasons for moving between areas in the United States were explored by two early studies on migration: The current population Sur-vey of October, 1946, and a study of Geographic Mobility and Employment Status conducted by the Census for the Bureau of Labor Statistics in March, 1963. Findings of both studies indicate that work related reasons are the most important in a decision to move. The percentage of male heads of families surveyed in the first study giving a particular reason for their move is as follows: 63.1 percent of moves were made either to take a job or to look for a job; 15 percent because of housing problems; 3.5 percent for change in marital status; 2.7 percent for health reasons; and 15.7 percent for other reasons. The distribution of reasons as given by males 18-64 in the 1963 Bureau of Labor Statistics Census study was as follows: 49.5 percent to take a job or look for work, and job transfer; 11.6 percent for marriage and family reasons; and 35.3 percent for other miscellaneous reasons.[57]

In another study conducted by Lansing and Mueller, who developed a better classification of reasons for moving, the reasons given by migrants were as follows: 58 percent for purely economic reasons; 14 percent for partly economic reasons (economic plus either family or community reasons or both); 23 percent for non-economic reasons; and 5 percent did not give any reason.[58] Pursuing the analysis further, Mueller states that "People between 35 and 55 are most likely to move for economic reasons only. Younger people often mentioned a combination of economic and non-economic incentives; like those in the middle age groups, they seldom move for non-economic reasons only. A sharp drop in economic reasons for moving in the 55-64 age groups is noteworthy."[59]

In a recent study by Johnson and Kiefert, 112 migrants gave twenty different reasons for moving. They are, in order of importance, as follows: wages were better, new community had better weather, more good job opportunities, more avenues to success and achievement, had relatives there, definite job offer, community was of desired size, community was a change of scenery, spouse wanted to move, had friends there, migrant felt he could better himself socially and culturally, could have improved position with the same employer, freedom of behavior, to go to school, military service, family conflict at home, better farm income, because parents moved, better chance to find someone to marry there, and fiance lived there.[60] Clearly, these reasons are not mutually exclusive; they can be grouped into fewer but broader categories similar to those mentioned above by Lansing and Mueller.

One major conclusion can be drawn from the findings on reasons for moving: both economic and non-economic motives are important factors in the decision to move, and an adequate and complete theory on migration should take into account both of these types of factors.

B.   Characteristics of Migrants

Two of the most important personal characteristics that are related to migration selectivity are age and education. Commenting on the importance of these factors, Lansing emphasizes that:

It is possible to examine one at a time the relation between measures of mobility and other socioeconomic characteristics of the population. Such an exercise, however, is of limited usefulness given the importance of age and education. Unless these two variables are somewhat taken into account it is difficult to draw conclusions about the importance of other characteristics known to be associated with age or with education or with both.[61]

16

It must be equally emphasized, however, that there are other socioeconomic characteristics that affect migration. Below are some of these
factors that research findings indicate influence spatial mobility.

Age

Migration selectivity by age is one of the most firmly established
migration differentials, which can be generalized over time, space, and
population, i.e., adolescent and young adults are more mobile than any
other age group.[62]

This generalization holds true for both individuals and families as
well as for international and internal migration. For example, between
two-thirds and four-fifths of the immigrants to the United States in the
nineteenth century were aged between 15 and 40 years;[63] and the median
ages of persons who had moved within the United States during the year
1949-1950 ranged from 19.8 to 30.5 years.[64]

Although people between the ages of fifteen and thirty-five are
more mobile than others, there is a variation in mobility within this
range. For example, in a study of migration in Japan, it was reported
that "The most mobile population over the years studied was at ages 10-
24, with maximum migration among the 15-19 age group. Occupational
migration among peasant boys and girls was impressive, but for the group
aged 25 and older net migration decreased sharply."[65] On the other
hand, Bogue reports that "...the stream of migrants arriving in a great
metropolis tends to be highly concentrated in the ages 20-29, whereas
the movement from the central city to the more distant suburbs tends to
be a phenomenon that has a very high incidence among parents just getting
their second or third child - ages 25-35."[66] Compare these findings with
those of Dorothy S. Thomas of internal migration in the United States.
She reports that the modal age for males traveling between urban areas is
30-34 years; 25-29 years for rural-nonfarm persons moving to urban or
rural-nonfarm destinations; and 20-24 years for rural-farm people going
to urban places and rural-nonfarm areas. Furthermore, Thomas notes that
the patterns for females tend to be similar to those of males, but to be
disproportionately concentrated among younger age groups.[67]

Various reasons are given for the high proportion of young adults in
migration: (1) young people are usually better able to adapt to new conditions involved at destination; (2) high school and college graduates go
for employment opportunities wherever these may be; (3) age is inseparably
linked to other factors such as tenure status, socioeconomic status,
wealth, marital status and number of children, and inertia all of which
are functionally related to spatial mobility.[68]

Education

The relation of education to migration also is one of the most supported generalizations. That is, highly educated people are more mobile than the less well-educated. Research findings by Brown and Hillery, Lansing and Mueller, Beshers and Nishiura, L. B. Brown, M. C. Brown, Brunner, Huie, Johnson and Kiefert, Ramsey and Anderson, and Tarver indicate a positive relationship between education and migration.[69] Exceptions to the above are reported by C. H. Brown,[70] and R. D. Geschwind and V. W. Ruttan.[71] They found no relationship between education and migration.

The most marked difference between education groups is that between those with college education and those with only a grade school or high school education. The difference in mobility rates between those with a grade school education and those who have been to high school are small, but on the average the latter are more mobile.[72]

The most evident reasons for the positive relationship between education and migration are that the highly educated and trained people are better equipped to compete for employment opportunities in other areas. This is specially true when one is considering the labor force in general and the movement of people between areas of varying economic and technical development. In like manner, the scattered findings of the negative relationships between education and migration may be interpreted in that the better educated are better equipped to compete for employment opportunities in the area of residence whenever such opportunities are available. In other words, the better educated and trained people have better competitive advantages than the less educated and trained for opportunities wherever these may be.

Familism and Family Considerations

Finds about the importance of family characteristics and considerations on decision to move are inconclusive and varied. For example, Jon Arno Doerflinger and Harry K. Schwarzweller conducted separately two research studies to determine the effects of family structure and family ties on migration. Doerflinger remarks that "Family structure was shown to have evolved from a more inclusive kin group which may have inhibited migration to the present form of nuclear family which may facilitate migration."[73] Schwarzweller, on the other hand, arrives at a somewhat different conclusion where he plays down the influence of familism and emphasizes the importance of other situational factors. He reports that "prior to migration, potential migrants and non-migrants apparently did not differ very greatly in family background characteristics or in their commitment to familistic norms; situationally-induced factors may have had more bearing upon an individual's decision to migrate than 'familism.'"[74] In pursuing the analysis further, Schwarzweller stresses the influence of family ties on stability and adjustment of migrants in the new community and on their yearning to go back to their original home community. He states:

> Going men who were separated by considerable distance from families-of-origin manifested greater feelings of residential instability than their counterparts, who lived nearer to parents...

> On the whole, the more familistic migrants, compared with their less familistic counterparts, tended to be tied into the societal structure to a lesser degree, in terms of their feelings about the new community as a place to live and their orientation to society as an abstract entity.[75]

Other studies by Brown, Schwarzweller, and Mangalam, and by Lansing and Mueller demonstrate the influence of family structure and separation of family members on migration. Brown, Schwarzweller, and Mangalam found that (1) members of the same extended family from three Eastern Kentucky neighborhoods tend to migrate to the same places and (2) migrants from these neighborhoods living in a given town are almost all related by close kinship ties.[76] The authors concluded "...that the consistency of the directional pattern of Eastern Kentucky's out- and in-migration may well be due to kinship relationships."[77] Later on they add: "Obviously when we have been saying that kinship ties have much to do with a Beech Creek migrant's destination, his ways of finding a job and a place to live in the new community, and his general social and personal adjustment, we have been emphasizing the continuing importance of the extended family."[78] In explaining the relationship between family structure and direction of migration the authors remark that:

> The kinship structure provides a highly permissive line of communication between kinsfolk in the home and the new communities which channels information about available job opportunities and living standards directly, and most meaningfully, to Eastern Kentucky families. Thus, kinship linkage tends to direct migrants to those areas where their kin groups are already established...

> Because of ascribed role of obligations, kinship structure also serves a protective function for new migrants to an area - a form of social insurance and a mechanism for smoother adaptation during the transitional phase of adjustment.[79]

Closely related to the above findings are those found by Lansing and Mueller regarding relationships between family ties and mobility. They report that of those who moved within five years, 25 percent gave family reasons for their move (4 percent for divorce, separation and to be farther from other family members, and 21 percent to be closer to relatives). Furthermore, people whose close relatives live in a different area are more likely to move than people who otherwise are similar but are not separated from their families. Of those who do move, 46 percent go to locations where there already is someone in their family. The reason given most often for their move is reunion with family members from whom they have been separated. Some of these moves involved a return to communities of previous residence where other family members were still living. The family ties of those who move to their relatives ease the task of moving. Relatives assist the migrant in a variety of ways: by providing job information, helping with the move, and generally by easing the process of settling into a new community.[80]

Two conclusions may be drawn from the above findings. First, family considerations play an important role in mobility: either to rejoin, or to be farther from, other family members, with the first being predominant. Secondly, although migrants go to places where some of family members already live, the underlying motivation may be wholly or partly economic in nature.

Marital Status, Sex, Race, and Intelligence

Research findings about the relationship between geographic mobility and marital status, sex, race, and intelligence vary from positive to zero to negative. For example, Schwarzweller, Duncan, and Brown report a positive relationship between mobility and marital status; that is, married people are more likely to migrate than single ones.[81] On the other hand, Bogue, Brown, Huie, and Johnson and Kiefert found a negative relationship between migration and marital status.[82]

Regarding sex and race, some studies show that females and Negroes are more mobile than males and whites,[83] while other studies show the reverse, that is, males and whites move more often than females and Negroes.[84] Still other studies show a zero relationship between migration and sex and race.[85]

As far as the impact of intelligence on migration is concerned, one can argue on a priori grounds that either the less or the more intelligent are more likely to migrate. For example, it may be argued that the ablest and most intelligent are better equipped to succeed and achieve satisfactory living conditions in their area of residence, and thus forcing the less intelligent to leave; it also can be argued that the more intelligent are more likely to respond to, and compete for, opportunities in other areas.

20

Studies on the impact of intelligence on migration show contradic-
tory results. A study by John Allen and others demonstrates a relationship between migration and intelligence.[86] Other studies by Petersen
and Brown indicate no relationship between the two. Furthermore, Petersen notes that selection depends more on conditions and opportunities at
destination than on those at the origin.[87] On the other hand, Sorokin
and Zimmerman note that cities attract the extremes while farms attract
the average strata in society. Likewise, Duncan proclaims that cities
attract the extremes of population in physical traits, social ranking
and intelligence.[88] Thomas was more accurate in explaining the relationships between intelligence and migration when he stated that no generalization at all can be made: "Migration may, under given circumstances,
select the intelligent; under other circumstances, the less intelligent;
and under still other circumstances, be quite unselective with regard to
intelligence."[89]

Occupation

The prominent theme here is that there is a direct relationship
between mobility and occupational skills. That is, persons with professional occupations are among the most migratory segments of the population, while laborers and operatives are among the least mobile.

First of all, it should be recognized that when we are talking
about occupational mobility, only those in the labor force are counted.
Here again, there are conflicting findings as to the level and direction
of relationship between migration and occupation, and, consequently, no
valid generalization can be made. For example, Thomlinson, Bogue, and
Lansing and Mueller report a positive relationship between mobility and
occupation.[90] On the other hand, Brunner states that "Nearby cities
attract disproportionately large proportions of unskilled workers from
rural America; more distant and larger cities, a higher proportion of
more capable and of professional workers."[91] Other studies on rural
migration report that farm to city movements are inversely associated
with tenure status; operators of small farms are more mobile than those
with larger holdings; and farmers and farm managers migrate less than
any other occupational category.[92]

C. Characteristics of and Conditions at Sending and Receiving Areas

Differences in characteristics which seem to influence migration
between sending and receiving areas have been measured in terms of
standard of living, economic activities, job opportunities, technological and industrial development, degree of urbanity, concentration of
population, and the "quality" of life in general. The assumption here

is that the general direction of migration is from areas of low standard of living, economic activities, job opportunities, technological and industrial development, degree of urbanity, "quality of life," and high concentration of population to areas more favored on these dimensions.[93] These relationships are implied by the push-pull hypothesis and the theory of intervening opportunities discussed earlier.

Although most of the above mentioned dimensions are not independent of one another, only job opportunities seem to hold valid over space and time, especially when those in the labor force are considered. The underlying assumption is that migration will take place when unemployment at the area of residence increases or when better employment opportunities at the area of destination become available or both. Ordinarily both - unemployment at the area of residence and employment opportunities at the area of destination - are present in migration. Very few of the studies have attempted to explain fully the interaction between these dual factors; instead, they considered one at a time. Some emphasized the importance of "push" factors[94] and others the "pull" factors.[95] Bishop states that "...a critical level of unemployment in terms of providing motivation for nonfarm migration develops when unemployment reaches 5 percent of the labor force..."[96] Likewise, Mueller notes: "As far as unemployment is concerned, comparisons of _actual_ unemployment rates of movers and non-movers before the move indicate that unemployment, particularly if it reaches the point of causing financial hardship, does make for moderately higher mobility."[97]

As regards the association between migration and the other characteristics of the sending and receiving areas - standard of living, technological and industrial development, degree of urbanity, and population concentration - in all probability the relationship does not hold over space and time. For example, the early movements of people from rural areas to urban centers occurred when the majority of population lived in rural areas and the minority in urban centers. Now that only 5.5 percent of the people live on farms, the past relationship is not as strong as it once was. Migration between urban areas and from urban centers to suburbs, and even to rural areas, is more common than migration from rural to urban areas. In regard to standard of living, technology, and industrialization as explanatory factors in migration, there is a different kind of problem. These factors do not provide a causal explanation of migration. People do not move to a higher standard of living or to an industry; they move to a new community, usually to take a new job. Thus, the availability of job opportunities is the underlying factor in such movements. The same is true of the early migration from Europe to the United States and the East-West settlements.

In regard to population density, it is sometimes thought that migration tends to take place from more to less densely populated areas;[98] but this assumption is questionable. The rural-urban movement is a case in point where the reverse takes place. Other factors such as resources, technology, industrialization and job opportunities must be taken into account; otherwise, population concentration per se offers very little explanation.

D. Others

Distance

Ravenstein in 1885 first noticed the inverse relationship between migration and distance. Undoubtedly, his formulations have had a profound influence upon many subsequent studies on migration. Almost each study takes distance, in one way or another, into account. In the 40's, two other scholars - George K. Zipf and Samuel A. Stouffer - each advanced mathematical formulae regarding migration and distance, which found wide acceptance among social scientists.

While Ravenstein and Zipf advocate a negative relationship between distance and mobility, Stouffer asserts that there is no necessary relationship between mobility and distance. Stouffer introduces opportunities and states that migration is directly proportional to the percentage increase in opportunities at that distance.[99]

Ravenstein gives no explanation for his "law" about the relationship between migration and distance. Zipf, on the other hand, explains the impact of distance on migration in terms of information and cost. First, gaining knowledge about conditions in areas of destination varies inversely in proportion to distance from the area of residence. And since, on the whole, information about conditions and events at a distance is prerequisite to a deliberate movement, gaining information will play a vital role in a great many problems that involve movement. Secondly, the actual expenditure, in terms of work, cost, etc., involved in any move is greater for long distances. And since it is man's nature to save cost and energy, short distance movements are more likely.[100]

According to Stouffer's theory of intervening opportunities, the relation between mobility and distance depends on an auxiliary relationship, which expresses the cumulated (intervening opportunities) as a function of distance.[101] In other words, opportunities are the reasons for which people move, and shorter distance moves are made only if similar opportunities are available.

Following Ravenstein, Zipf, and Stouffer's generalizations about geographical mobility and distance, numerous studies have been conducted about this subject. Below is a sample of their findings.

1. "While a majority of migrating youth in their first move settle near their parents' home, the better educated go farther."[102]

2. "The greater the distance a migrant moves, the more likely it is that his destination is a large city."[103]

3. "The youth of tenant families are more mobile than those of owner families, but they move shorter distances."[104]

4. "Males, though less migratory than females, travel farther."[105]

5. "Nearby cities attract disproportionately large proportions of unskilled workers from rural America; more distant and larger cities a higher proportion of more capable and of professional workers."[106]

6. "The short distance, local movements...do not seem to obey any law of direction."[107]

7. "As soon as movements become long enough in distance to transcend locality boundaries, they begin to assume regularities and uniformities."[108]

8. "Most people go a short distance; few people go a long distance."[109]

9. "Girls were more apt than boys to travel farther."[110]

10. "The longer the distance migrated the more likely a family was to have made several previous moves."

11. "The longer the distance migrated the higher the family income tended to be."

12. "The longer the distance migrated the more likely a wage earner was to have sought job information from formal sources, and he was more likely to have contracted for a job before moving."[111]

13. "Movement from nonfarm to farm residence involved more distance, on the average, than other types of migration."[112]

14. "Where good town jobs are scarce, rural people emigrate abroad."[113]

15. Intrastate migration is higher than interstate migration.[114]

Communication

An important, but neglected, factor in the study of migration is communication. Regardless of the reason or reasons for which a person moves from one area to another, he must have some information about the conditions in the area of destination before he makes his move. Migrants do not move blindly and randomly between areas. Except in the case of forced migration, migrants choose the area that is most suitable to them based on information they have.

Acquisition of information about conditions in destination areas may be of various sources: direct personal contact and knowledge, relatives, friends, government or private agencies, newspapers, magazines, radio, T.V., etc. It is this type of information that is implied in "awareness of better opportunities elsewhere" of the push-pull theory and Zipf's hypothesis.

Among the few research studies that addressed themselves to the communication problem, all indicate a positive relationship between migration and prior favorable information about the area of destination.[115]

Stream and Counterstream

The fact that each migration stream produces a counterstream has been noted and confirmed by Ravenstein, Lee, Bogue, and Brown and Hillery,[116] to mention a few. Unfortunately, none of the studies pursues the matter further to describe the differences, if there are any, between the migrants in the two streams or the reasons for which they moved in and out. For example, do migrants in both streams have similar socioeconomic characteristics? If yes, why then does one stream go in while another goes out? If not, on what basis was differentiation made between migrants and non-migrants in past studies? Did they consider only one stream of migrants? Which one? Furthermore, what were the reasons that led one group to leave and the other to move in? If the movement was for better conditions and opportunities for one stream of migrants, how come the stream is not true for the other stream of migrants? If these various questions and others were followed in the study of stream and counterstream, our understanding of the migration phenomenon could have gained and improved tremendously. In fact, it is the writer's feeling that a well-planned study in this area will yield more information and offer a better explanation of the factors underlying migration than most of the other fragmented studies done on migration so far.

Summary and Conclusion

Past theories and research studies have tended to focus on a variety of factors to explain and predict migration. These factors included reasons for moving, personal characteristics, characteristics of and conditions at sending and receiving areas, and other miscellaneous variables such as distance, communication, and streams and counterstreams.

Each theory, hypothesis, law, and variable has been tested a number of times. The most valid and established relationships that seem to hold over time and space are:

1. Predominance of the economic motive: the percentage of those who move for economic reasons is higher than for any other purposes.

2. Education and age: migration is positively related to education; and those who are between eighteen and thirty-five years old are more migratory than any other age group.

3. "Opportunities" of a non-economic kind at the area of destination: awareness of better opportunities at receiving area is positively related to migration.

4. Communication and streams and counterstreams: importance of acquisition of information about conditions in receiving areas prior to move; and each stream produces a counterstream.

Findings about the association between migration and the other factors were varied and many times contradictory. They vacillated between positive, zero, and negative. If we are to follow the tenet of science in that no definite number of studies can prove a case, but one study can disprove it, then we cannot claim much about having established "laws" of migration. If this is the case, where do we stand on migration? Is it lawless, unpatterned, and random as some researchers had already claimed it to be? These questions cannot be answered satisfactorily here; they will be elaborated upon toward the end of this paper. It must be mentioned, however, that the inconsistencies in the evidence could be due to one or a combination of the following factors:

1. Faulty methodology.

2. Differences in measurement of concepts or cutting points.

3. Differences in populations studied.

4. Differences in population with which the migrants were compared: population of sending area, receiving area, or the entire population.

5. Types of variables considered and controlled.

6. Overgeneralization of theories and hypotheses.

7. Deviant cases.

8. Spurious relationship.

The results of migration studies clearly indicate that many factors are involved in decision to move. Some of these factors are causal ones, others are conditional, and others are spuriously related to migration. A full understanding and adequate explanation of the migration process requires that these factors be identified and that their independent and combined effects be specified. Unless this is done, explanation of migration will be incomplete, and prediction uncertain. It is only when we consider all factors simultaneously that we will be able to evaluate the importance of each factor as well as specify the necessary and sufficient conditions under which migration will or will not take place.

It is safe to say that previous research studies were on the whole descriptive rather than explanatory.[117] Further studies should concentrate on explanation if progress is to be made for understanding and explaining the migration process. Furthermore, there has been a tendency, which has been gaining acceptance and status among certain prominent demographers, to describe mobility in terms of mathematical "formulae" by using certain high predictor variables, regardless of the relevancy of these variables to explaining and comprehending migration. Zipf's hypothesis and Stouffer's theory of intervening opportunities are two cases in point. These formulations enabled some researchers to obtain a correlation between expected and observed migrants as high as .90.[118] As a descriptive and predictive device such hypotheses and formulae are quite adequate, but they do not necessarily tell us about the causes of migration. Their power of explanation is no better than predicting the number of people who move into and out of a given community from the number of cars that enter and leave this community, but this approach does not tell us anything about reasons underlying the movement.

A final important note should be made regarding the development of theory and research in migration. These two phases of science, which are supposed to interact and benefit from and build upon one another,[119] have been greatly neglected. On the whole, migration theory and research evolved independently from one another, and consequently we have speculative theories and sterile ad hoc research. For example, on one hand we find a tremendous amount of data from thousands of research studies of various disciplines remaining fragmented and without any general explanatory system as a binder for their diverse findings. The various theories, on the other hand, remain unmodified as they were originally proposed - either narrow in scope or at such a high level of abstraction that they cannot be tested - in spite of the mounting evidence which contradicts their assumptions. The field of migration as it exists today, with theories that do not explain and assumptions that cannot be measured or invalidated when tested, and with an excessive amount of data that are not integrated into any unified framework for dealing meaningfully with migration, would not, as Hauser noted, merit the appellation of a science. Unfortunately, there is still too much of a tendency among migration students to produce discrete and descriptive studies with little or no attention to theoretical framework as a basis for their orientation or for the formulation of their conclusions. In view of the tremendous accumulation of data about migration, it seems that enough is now known about the migration phenomenon to direct our energies to integration of theory and research and the development of a comprehensive theoretical framework.[120] Such a theoretical framework should be predicated on the following:

1. All meaningfully related factors that research has demonstrated to be associated with migration.

2. Refine the lists of factors into meaningful categories and/or indexes that can be empirically verified.

3. Specify the types of factors - causal, precipitants, intervening, control, and dependent variables - and their independent as well as interdependent relationships to migration. These relationships should be stated in a verifiable way.

4. Indicate the gap of knowledge in any area.

5. Leave the door open for additional variables that future research may discover to be important in migration.

Footnotes

1. E. G. Ravenstein, "The Laws of Migration," _Journal of the Royal Statistical Society_, XLVIII, 2 (June, 1885), pp. 167-227.

2. E. G. Ravenstein, "The Laws of Migration," _Journal of the Royal Statistical Society_, LII (June, 1889), pp. 241-301.

3. _Ibid._, p. 286.

4. _Ibid._, XLVIII, pp. 198-99.

5. <u>Ibid.</u>, LII, p. 286.

6. <u>Ibid.</u>, XLVIII, p. 198.

7. <u>Ibid.</u>, p. 199.

8. <u>Ibid.</u>, LII, p. 287.

9. <u>Ibid.</u>, XLVIII, p. 199.

10. <u>Ibid.</u>

11. <u>Ibid.</u>, LII, p. 288.

12. See, e.g., Theodore Anderson, "Intermetropolitan Migration: A Correlation Analysis," <u>The American Journal of Sociology</u>, LXI (March, 1956), pp. 459-62; Glenn V. Fuguit, "Part-Time Farming and the Push-Pull Hypothesis," <u>The American Journal of Sociology</u>, LXIV (January, 1959), pp. 375-79; Julius Isaac, <u>Economics of Migration</u> (London, 1967); Carter Goodrich and others, <u>Migration and Economic Opportunity</u> (Philadelphia, 1936); Dorothy Swaine Thomas, <u>Social and Economic Aspects of Swedish Population Movement</u> (New York, 1942); John B. Lansing and Eva Mueller, <u>The Geographic Mobility of Labor</u> (Ann Arbor, Michigan, 1967).

13. Donald J. Bogue, "Internal Migration," <u>The Study of Population</u>, eds., Philip Hauser and Otis Dudley Duncan (Chicago: University of Chicago Press, 1959), p. 502, citing George Kingsley Zipf, <u>Human Behavior and the Principle of Least Effort</u> (Cambridge, Massachusetts, 1949).

14. <u>Ibid.</u>

15. <u>Ibid.</u>

16. Samuel A. Stouffer, "Intervening Opportunities: A Theory Relating Mobility and Distance," <u>American Sociological Review</u>, V (December, 1940), pp. 845-67. Stouffer gives the following mathematical formulation for his theory, a formula that apparently impressed most demographers and made this theory famous: $y_s = a \frac{x_s}{x}$.

y = the number of persons moving from an origin to a circular band of width Δs, its inner boundary being S-1/2 Δs units of distance from the origin or center of the circle and its outer boundary being S+1/2 Δs units from the origin.
x = the number of intervening opportunities, that is, the cumulated number of opportunities between the origin and distance S.
Δx = the number of opportunities within the band of width Δx.

17. _Ibid._, pp. 854-56.

18. Lansing and Mueller, op. cit., p. 5. See also Lloyd Reynolds, _The Structure of Labor Markets_, 1951; Michael J. Brennan, "Regional Labor and Capital Migration" (Unpublished Report, Brown University, 1967).

19. Everett S. Lee, "A Theory of Migration," _Demography_, 52, III (1966).

20. _Ibid._

21. _Ibid._

22. _Ibid._

23. _Ibid._

24. _Ibid._, p. 54.

25. _Ibid._

26. _Ibid._, p. 55.

27. _Ibid._

28. _Ibid._

29. _Ibid._

30. _Ibid._, p. 56.

31. _Ibid._

32. _Ibid._

33. _Ibid._

34. _Ibid._

35. _Ibid._

36. _Ibid._, p. 57.

37. _Ibid._

38. Bogue, "Internal Migration," _op. cit._, pp. 486-509.

39. <u>Ibid.</u>, p. 502, citing G. K. Zipf, <u>Human Behavior and the Principle of Least Effort</u> (Cambridge, Massachusetts, 1949).

40. <u>Ibid.</u>

41. <u>Ibid.</u>

42. Bogue, "Internal Migration," <u>op. cit.</u>, p. 502, citing A. R. Mangus and R. L. McNamara, <u>Levels of Living and Population Movements in Rural Areas in Ohio, 1930-40</u>, Ohio Agricultural Experiment Station Bulletin, 639 (Wooster, Ohio, 1943); J. K. Folger, "Some Aspects of Migration in the Tennessee Valley,"<u>American Sociological Review</u>, XVIII (1953), pp. 253-60.

43. Bogue, "Internal Migration," <u>op. cit.</u>, p. 502, citing J. Folger, "Some Aspects of Migration in the Tennessee Valley," <u>American Sociological Review</u>, XVIII (1953), pp. 253-60.

44. Bogue, "Internal Migration," <u>op. cit.</u>, p. 502, citing Stouffer, <u>op. cit.</u>

45. Bogue, "Internal Migration," <u>op. cit.</u>, p. 502; Donald J. Bogue and Margaret Marman Hagood, <u>Subregional Migration in the United States, 1935-1940</u> (Miami, Ohio, 1953), Vol. II, <u>Differential Migration in the Corn and Cotton Belts</u>, Scripps Foundation Studies in Population Distribution, No. 6, pp. 124-27.

46. Bogue, "Internal Migration," <u>op. cit.</u>, p. 502, citing Donald J. Bogue and others, <u>Subregional Migration in the United States, 1935-1940</u> (Oxford, Ohio, 1957), Vol. I, <u>Streams of Migration</u>, Scripps Foundation Distribution, No. 5.

47. Bogue, "Internal Migration," <u>op. cit.</u>, p. 502.

48. <u>Ibid.</u>

49. <u>Ibid.</u>, p. 503.

50. <u>Ibid.</u>, citing H. S. Shyrock, Jr. and Hope, T. Eldridge, "Internal Migration in Peace and War," <u>American Sociological Review</u>, XII (1947), pp. 27-39.

51. William Petersen, <u>Population</u> (New York, 1961), pp. 606-07.

52. *Ibid*., pp. 607-09. According to Petersen, innovating migration refers to those persons who leave as a means of achieving new conditions. Conservative migration, on the other hand, refers to those persons who respond to a change in conditions by trying to retain what they have had, moving geographically in order to remain where they are in all other respects.

53. Robert McGinnis, "Randomization and Inferences in Sociological Research," <u>American Sociological Review</u>, XXII (October, 1957), p. 411. McGinnis distinguishes between three types of hypotheses: <u>absolute</u>, <u>finitely conditional</u>, and <u>infinitely conditional</u>. An <u>absolute hypothesis</u> does not establish conditions regarding the relation of the variables under consideration. A <u>finitely conditional hypothesis</u> requires a condition of statistical independence between X, Y and a finite number of other variables, Z_i, if the hypothesis is to be true. An <u>infinitely conditional hypothesis</u> specifies conditions for the variables X, Y and infinite number of variables Z_i. The first hypothesis, absolute, is referred to as "descriptive," and no causation is established; the third, infinitely conditional, as "explanatory," and absolute causation is established; while the second falls somewhere in between the two.

54. William Petersen, <u>Population</u> (New York, 1961), p. 619.

55. Bogue, "Internal Migration," <u>op. cit</u>., p. 504. Bogue states that the first migration differential has been valid in many places and over long periods of time. The other five differentials are valid at the present time in the United States population.

56. Edmund de S. Brunner, <u>The Growth of a Science: A Half-Century of Rural Sociological Research in the U.S</u>. (New York, 1957), pp. 54-55.

57. Lansing and Mueller, op. cit., pp. 36-38, citing Special Labor Force Report, <u>Geographic Mobility and Employment Status</u>, March 1962 and March 1963, Bureau of Labor Statistics, May, 1964.

58. Lansing and Mueller, <u>op. cit</u>., p. 38. Lansing mentions that the more intensive discussion of reasons for moving had the effect of increasing the proportion of moves for which an economic reason was given.

59. *Ibid*., p. 59.

60. Ronald L. Johnson and James J. Kiefert, "Factors Involved in the Decision to Migrate and the Impact of Migration Upon the Individual and the Sender and Receiver Community" (Unpublished Report, University of North Dakota, 1968), pp. 8-9.

61. Lansing and Mueller, op. cit., p. 44.

62. Bogue, "Internal Migration," op. cit., p. 504; James S. Brown and George A. Hillery, Jr., "The Great Migration, 1940-1960," The Southern Appalachian Region, ed., Thomas Ford (Lexington, 1962), p. 67; Petersen, op. cit., p. 593; Johnson and Kiefert, op. cit., pp. 19-20; Brunner, op. cit., p. 54; Otis Durant Duncan, "The Theory and Consequences of Mobility of Farm Population," ed., Joseph J. Spengler and Otis Dudley Duncan (Glencoe, Ill., 1956), pp. 423-432; Lansing and Mueller, op. cit., p. 335; Dorothy S. Thomas, "Age and Economic Differentials in Internal Migration in the United States: Structure and Distance," International Population Conference (Vienna, 1959), pp. 714-19; Mangalam, op. cit., p. 31, citing James M. Beshers and Eleanor N. Nishiura, "A Theory of Internal Migration Differentials," Social Forces, XXXIX (March, 1961), pp. 214-18; Mangalam, op. cit., p. 30, citing Ward W. Bauder, "Analysis of Trends in Population, Population Characteristics, and Community Life in Southern Iowa" (Seminar on Adjustment and Its Problems in Southern Iowa, Iowa State University, College of Agriculture, 1959), pp. 113-37; Mangalam, op. cit., p. 36, citing Phillips H. Brown and John M. Petersen, "The Exodus from Arkansas," Arkansas Economist, II (Winter, 1960), pp. 10-15; Mangalam, op. cit., p. 57, citing Yoskiko Kasahara, "The Influx and Exodus of Migrants Among 47 Prefectures in Japan, 1920-1935" (Unpublished Doctoral Dissertation, University of Michigan, 1958); Mangalam, op. cit., p. 89, citing Dorothy Swaine Thomas, "Age and Economic Differentials in Interstate Migration," Population Index, XXIV (October, 1958), pp. 313-25.

63. Petersen, op. cit., p. 593, citing Imre Ferenczi, International Migrations, I, Statistics (New York, 1929), pp. 212-13.

64. Petersen, op. cit., p. 593, citing Otis Dudley Duncan and Albert J. Reiss, Jr., Social Characteristics of Urban and Rural Communities, 1950 (New York, 1956), pp. 83-87.

65. Mangalam, op. cit., p. 57, citing Yoshiko Kasahara, op. cit.

66. Bogue, "Internal Migration," op. cit., p. 504.

67. Thomas, "Age and Economic Differentials in Internal Migration in the United States: Structure and Distance," op. cit., pp. 718-719.

68. See, for example, Petersen, op. cit., p. 593; Duncan, op. cit., p. 423; Bogue, "Internal Migration," op. cit., p. 504.

69. Brown and Hillery, op. cit., p. 68; Lansing and Mueller, op. cit., p. 335; James D. Tarver, "Predicting Migration," Social Forces, XXXIX (March, 1961), p. 210; Brunner, op. cit.; Johnson and Kiefert, op. cit., pp. 19-20; Mangalam, op. cit., p. 31, citing Beshers and Nishiura, pp. 214-18; Mangalam, op. cit., p. 36, citing L. B. Brown, "English Migrants to New Zealand: The Decision to Move," Human Relations (May, 1960), pp. 167-74; Mangalam, op. cit., p. 36, citing Morgan C. Brown, "Selected Characteristics of Southern Rural Negroes Exchanged to a Southern Urban Center," Rural Sociology, XXVII (March, 1962), pp. 63-70; Mangalam, op. cit., p. 52, citing J. M. Huie, "Migration of Rural Residents," Alabama Agricultural Experiment Station Highlights of Agricultural Research, IX (Summer, 1962), 14; Mangalam, op. cit., p. 74, citing C. E. Ramsey and W. A. Anderson, Migration of the New York State Population, Cornell Agricultural Experiment Station (Ithaca, 1958).

70. Mangalam, op. cit., p. 35, citing Claude Harold Brown, "Personal and Social Characteristics Associated with Migrants Status Among Adult Males from Rural Pennsylvania" (Unpublished Doctoral Dissertation, Pennsylvania State University, 1960). The study was conducted on young adult males from rural areas.

71. Mangalam, op. cit., p. 46, citing R. D. Geschwind and V. W. Ruttan, Job Mobility and Migration in a Low Income Rural Community, Indiana Agricultural Experiment Station (1961). In this case, migration was measured in terms of job mobility.

72. Lansing and Mueller, op. cit., pp. 336-37.

73. Jon Arno Doerflinger, "Patterns of Internal Migration Related to Institutional and Age-Sex Structure of the U.S.," Dissertation Abstracts (Unpublished Doctoral Dissertation, University of Wisconsin, 1962), p. 2238.

74. Harry K. Schwarzweller, Family Ties, Migration and Transitional Adjustment of Young Men from Eastern Kentucky, University of Kentucky Agricultural Experiment Station (Lexington, 1964), p. 38.

75. Ibid., pp. 38-39.

76. James S. Brown and others, "Kentucky Mountain Migration and the Stem-Family: An American Variation on a Theme by LePlay," Rural Sociology, XXVIII (March, 1963), pp. 48-69.

77. Ibid., p. 48.

78. Ibid., p. 68.

79.   _Ibid._, pp. 53-54.

80.   Lansing and Mueller, _op. cit._, pp. 125-135.

81.   Schwarzweller, _op. cit._, p. 24; Duncan, _op. cit._, pp. 426-32; Mangalam, _op. cit._, p. 35, citing Claude Harold Brown, _op. cit._

82.   Johnson and Kiefert, _op. cit._, pp. 19-20; Mangalam, _op. cit._, p. 33, citing Donald J. Bogue, "International Migration and National Origins of the Population," _The Population of the United States_ (Glencoe, Illinois, 1959); Mangalam, _op. cit._, p. 36, citing L. B. Brown, "English Migrants to New Zealand: The Decision to Move," _op. cit._, _Human Relations_, XIII (May, 1960), pp. 167-74; Mangalam, _op. cit._, p. 52, citing Marie Brase Hotz, "A Study of Cohort Migration in the U.S.: 1870-1950" (Unpublished Doctoral Dissertation, Washington University, 1955).

83.   Brown and Hillery, _op. cit._, p. 67; Mangalam, _op. cit._, p. 34, citing Gladys K. Bowles, _Farm Population...Net Migration from Rural-Farm Population, 1940-1950_, Agricultural Marketing Service (n.p., 1956); Edmund de S. Brunner, _op. cit._, pp. 34-37; Duncan, _op. cit._, pp. 426-32; Mangalam, _op. cit._, p. 36, citing Phillips H. Brown and John M. Petersen, _op. cit._

84.   Bogue, "International Migration," _op. cit._, p. 504; Mangalam, _op. cit._, citing L. B. Brown, _op. cit._, pp. 167-74; Mangalam, _op. cit._, p. 57, Kashahara, _op. cit._; Dorothy Swaine Thomas, "Age and Economic Differentials in Interstate Migration," _op. cit._; Lansing and Mueller, _op. cit._, p. 343.

85.   Mangalam, _op. cit._, p. 52, citing Huie, _op. cit._, p. 14; Mangalam, _op. cit._, p. 74, citing C. E. Ramsey and W. A. Anderson, _op. cit._; Mangalam, _op. cit._, p. 50, citing C. Horace Hamilton and Herbert Aurbach, _What's Happening to North Carolina Farms and Farmers_, North Carolina Agricultural Experiment Station (n.p., 1958).

86.   Mangalam, _op. cit._, p. 26, citing John H. Allen and others, _Pulling Up Stakes and Breaking Apron Strings: A Study of Mobility Among Pennsylvania's Rural Youth_, Pennsylvania Agricultural Experiment Station (n.p., 1955).

87.   Petersen, _op. cit._, pp. 101-02; Mangalam, _op. cit._, p. 35; Claude Harold Brown, _op. cit._

88.   A Sorokin and Carle C. Zimmerman, _Principles of Rural-Urban Sociology_ (New York, 1929), p. 571; Mangalam, _op. cit._, p. 42, citing Duncan, _op. cit._

89. Petersen, op. cit., p. 602, citing Dorothy Swaine Thomas, Migration Differentials (n.p., n.d.), p. 125.

90. Bogue, "Internal Migration," op. cit., p. 55; Lansing and Mueller, op. cit., p. 336; Johnson and Kiefert, op. cit., p. 1, citing Ralph Thomlinson, Population Dynamics: Causes and Consequences of World Demographic Change (New York, 1965).

91. Brunner, op. cit., p. 54.

92. Ibid., p. 58; Duncan, op. cit., p. 423; Mangalam, op. cit., p. 31, citing Beshers and Nishiura, op. cit.

93. See, for example, Brown and others, op. cit., pp. 52-53; Brown and Hillery, op. cit., p. 73; Mangalam, op. cit., p. 31, citing C. E. Bishop, "Economic Aspects of Migration from Farms," Farm Policy Forum, XIII (n.d., 1960-61), pp. 14-20; Mangalam, op. cit., p. 26, citing Allen and others, op. cit.; Mangalam, op. cit., p. 28, citing Frank T. Bachmura, "Migration and Factor Adjustment in Lower Mississippi Valley Agriculture, 1940-50," Journal of Farm Economics, XXXVIII (November, 1956), pp. 1024-42; Bogue, "Internal Migration," op. cit., p. 486; Mangalam, op. cit., p. 35, citing J. Norma, "Association of Selected Socio-Economic Characteristics with Net Migration from Three Kentucky Economic Areas, 1920-1950" (Unpublished Masters Thesis, University of Kentucky, 1958); Mangalam, op. cit., p. 36, citing Brown and Petersen, op. cit.; Brunner, op. cit., p. 55; Mangalam, op. cit., p. 38, citing Benecio T. Catapusan and Flora E. Diaz Catapusan, "Displaced Migrant Families in Rural Philippines," Sociology and Social Research, XL (January-February, 1956), pp. 186-89; Doerflinger, op. cit., p. 41; Duncan, op. cit., p. 21; Mangalam, op. cit., p. 47, citing Harold Frank Goldsmith, "The Meaning of Migration: A Study of the Migration Expectation of High School Students" (Unpublished Doctoral Dissertation, Michigan State University, 1962); George A. Hillery and others, "Migration Systems of the Southern Appalachians: Some Demographic Observations," Rural Sociology, XXX (March, 1965), pp. 33-48; Mangalam, op. cit., p. 50, citing Hamilton and Aurbach, op. cit.; Johnson and Kiefert, op. cit., p. 19; Mangalam, op. cit., p. 57, citing T. Kempinski, "Rural Migration," Rural Sociology, XXVI (March, 1961), pp. 70-73; Lansing and Mueller, op. cit., p. 85; Clarence Senior, "Migration as a Process and Migrant as a Person," Population Review, VI (January, 1962), pp. 33-34; Tarver, op. cit., p. 213.

94. See, for example, Kashara, op. cit., p. 57.

95. See, for example, Petersen, op. cit., pp. 602-03.

96. Mangalam, op. cit., p. 32, citing Bishop, op. cit.

97. Lansing and Mueller, op. cit., p. 85.

98. Horace Hamilton, "Population Pressure and Other Factors Affecting Net Rural-Urban Migration," Population Theory and Policy, eds., Joseph J. Spengler and Otis Dudley Duncan (Glencoe, Ill., 1956), pp. 419-24.

99. The formulations and assumptions advanced by Ravenstein, Zipf, and Stouffer have been elaborated upon in details earlier.

100. Zipf, Human Behavior and the Principle of Least Effort, op. cit.

101. Stouffer, "Intervening Opportunities: A Theory Relating Mobility and Distance," op. cit., pp. 846-47.

102. Brunner, op. cit., p. 54.

103. Ibid.

104. Ibid.

105. Ibid., p. 55.

106. Ibid.

107. Duncan, op. cit., p. 420.

108. Ibid., p. 421.

109. Stouffer, "Intervening Opportunities: A Theory Relating Mobility and Distance," op. cit., p. 845.

110. Mangalam, op. cit., p. 26, citing Allen and others, op. cit.

111. Mangalam, op. cit., p. 41, citing Alfred Mascey Denton, "Some Factors in the Migration of Construction Workers" (Unpublished Doctoral Dissertation, University of North Carolina, 1960).

112. Mangalam, op. cit., p. 74, citing Ramsey and Anderson, op. cit.

113. Mangalam, op. cit., p. 57, citing Kempenski, op. cit.

114. Brown and Hillery, op. cit., pp. 63-66.

115. Alan Richardson, "Some Psychological Aspects of British Emigration to Australia," British Journal of Sociology, X (December, 1959), pp. 327-37; Mangalam, op. cit., p. 41, citing Denton, op. cit.; Mangalam, op. cit., p. 35, citing Breazeale, op. cit.; Mangalam, op. cit., p. 36, citing L. B. Brown, op. cit.; Mangalam, op. cit., p. 46, citing Geschwind and Ruttan, op. cit.

116. Ravenstein, LII, op. cit., p. 287; Lee, op. cit., p. 54; Bogue, "Internal Migration," op. cit., p. 502; Brown and Hillery, op. cit., pp. 61-63.

117. The difference between descriptive and explanatory study or hypothesis is that in the latter case all known variables to be related to the independent variable(s) are controlled, while a limited number of no control variables are considered in the former. This matter was explained in more detail earlier in this chapter.

118. John R. Folger, "Models in Migration," Selected Studies of Migration Since World War II (New York, 1958), pp. 156-57.

119. See, for example, William J. Goode and Paul K. Hatt, Methods in Social Research (New York, 1952), pp. 8-16. Goode and Hatt outlined five contributions of theory to research and five contributions of research to theory. They state: "Theory is a tool of science in these ways: (1) it defines the major orientation of a science, by defining the kinds of data which are to be abstracted; (2) it offers a conceptual scheme by which the relevant phenomena are systemized, classified, and interrelated; (3) it summarizes facts into (a) empirical generalizations and (b) systems of generalizations; (4) it predicts facts; and (5) it points to gaps in our knowledge.

"On the other hand, facts are also productive of theory in these ways: (1) facts help to initiate theories; (2) they lead to the reformulation of existing theory; (3) they cause the rejection of theories which do not fit the facts; (4) they change the focus and orientation of theory; and (5) they clarify and redefine theory."

120. See, for example, Philip M. Hauser, "Present Status and Prospects of Research in Population," Population Theory and Policy, eds., Joseph J. Spengler and Otis Dudley Duncan (Glencoe, Illinois, 1956), pp. 70-85; Rupert B. Vance, "Is Theory for Demographers?" Social Forces, XXXI (October, 1952), pp. 9-13.

CHAPTER III

THEORETICAL FRAMEWORK

The purpose of this chapter is to formulate a comprehensive and integrated theoretical framework of migration that is amenable to empirical verification. The theoretical model presented below grows out of our analysis of the migration theories and research discussed previously in Chapter II. But in contrast to the macro and partial theories discussed earlier, this theory is: (1) more comprehensive in that it deals with the entire decision-making process to migrate and includes the major factors relating to the various stages of the migration process; and (2) it is applicable to individual units rather than to categories or classes of people. Furthermore, the model is open to the possibility of additional variables that future research may prove to be important in migration.

The basic assumptions of the present theory are: predisposition to move and actual migration are responses to the migrant's perceived unmet needs and wants in the area of residence and to the existing opportunities in the area of destination to meet these unmet needs and wants. Personal, community, and situational factors affect the magnitude of the migrant's perception of his deprivation, his predisposition to move, and his ability to migrate.

In order to develop the above statement into a meaningful and verifiable theoretical framework of migration, the following questions will have to be answered. What are the migrant's needs and wants? What are those personal, community, and situational factors that affect migrant's perception of his deprivation, his predisposition to migrate, and his ability to move? How do these factors enter into the decision-making process to move? What are the causal, limiting, and facilitating factors for migration?

If the migrant is to be the unit of analysis, then the migrant's goals or reasons for moving[1] should be assumed as the basic causal factors of migration; and all other factors relating to migration - personal, community, and situational - should be viewed as facilitating or inhibiting conditions of migration.[2] Accordingly, migration is a form of purposive behavior, and the decision-making process to move will be viewed as a deliberate action whereby the migrant weighs the advantages and disadvantages of his move, and that decision to move will be reached when the individual feels that his gains will outweigh his losses. It must be noted, however, that decision to move is not necessarily rational. For it is not so much the actual conditions at areas of origin and destination as the perception of these conditions by the migrant that results in migration. In other words, the migrant's evaluation of these conditions may or may not correspond with the actual ones, and the migrant's decision to move may or may not result in a net total gain. A migrant often moves only to find himself in a "worse" condition than before. Commenting on the subjectivity of decision to move, Mangalam states that "...a decision to move is a highly subjective act. It is subjective in that a high degree of deprivation in certain values as well as blocking of all the means for overcoming them need only to be felt by the collectivity, whether or not objective evidence exists for that feeling."[3] In like manner, Runciman asserts that "Relative deprivation should always be understood to mean a _sense_ of deprivation; a person who is relatively 'deprived' need not be 'objectively' deprived in the more usual sense that he is demonstrably lacking something."[4]

Stages of the Migration Process

The migration phenomenon here is conceptualized as a process composed of three stages: deprivation, predisposition to move, and migration. Each stage is a necessary but not sufficient condition to the stage following it.

It is assumed that perception of deprivation is affected by exogenous factors, which will not be dealt with in this study. Predisposition to move, on the other hand, is a function of felt deprivation: dissatisfaction with one's wants in the area of residence and perception of opportunities in the area of destination to satisfy these wants - employment opportunities, education, facilities, health facilities, social ties, housing facilities, and climate.[5] The effects of felt deprivation on predisposition to move may be explained by the theory of relative deprivation outlined by Runciman:[6] "A is relatively deprived of X when (1) he does not have X, (2) he sees some other person, which may include himself at some previous or expected time, as having X (whether or not this is or will be in fact the case), (3) he wants X, and (4) it is feasible for him to have X."[7] Underlying the notion of relative deprivation is that when a person finds his needs and wants are not being fulfilled, he experiences unpleasant or painful tension which in turn induces the person to alter his situation. One way of doing this will be for the individual to acquire the thing he needs or wants.

The principle of relative deprivation operates on predisposition to migrate in the following way: a person who feels that his needs and wants (employment opportunities, health facilities, educational facilities, housing, social ties, and climate) are not being satisfied, and who becomes aware of better opportunities in another area, will be motivated to move.

Not all persons desiring to move, however, will or can migrate. Actual migration is affected by the desire to move and several other factors, each of which acts independently or in combination with other factors to facilitate or limit mobility, depending on the type of migration (general migration and migration for employment purposes). These factors are: education, age, economic status, professional skills, family size, liquidity assets, and sex. It is assumed that economic status, family size, and fixed assets, affect all types of migration - general migration. Education, age, sex, and professional skills are most important for individuals seeking employment opportunities. The nature of relationships between these factors and migration are discussed below.

A. <u>General Migration</u>. The effects of economic status, family size, and liquidity of assets upon general migration is related to the cost of moving. Unless a person has the money or can borrow it, he cannot move.

The effect of family size on migration is that the cost of the move increases with increase in family size.

Possession of fixed assets such as land and house represent another obstacle for the migrant, for in areas of high out-migration he may have to sell at a loss.

Thus, general migration is expected to be positively related to economic status and liquidity of assets, and negatively related to family size.

B. <u>Migration for Employment Purposes</u>. The effects of education, age, employment status, professional skills, and sex on migration may be explained in that those with better education and professional skills are in a better position to compete for available jobs at the area of destination.

Regarding the influence of age on migration, it is felt that the young, specially those entering the labor market - high school and college graduates - are more likely to seek their fortune in another area than to compete with the already established people who usually are older. Furthermore, younger persons are usually less attached to their community

41

FIGURE 1

THE THREE STAGES OF VOLUNTARY MIGRATION:
DEPRIVATION, PREDISPOSITION TO MOVE, AND MIGRATION

I   II   III

Exogenous or
Antecedent Variables ———→ Deprivation ———→ Predisposition to Move ———→ Migration

Community Support System:
General availability of
employment opportunities,
education facilities,
health facilities, housing
facilities, social ties,
and climate, etc.

1. Dissatisfaction at
   area of residence with
   employment opportunities,
   education facilities,
   health facilities, social
   ties, housing, and climate

2. Awareness of feasibility
   at destination of employment opportunities, education facilities, health
   facilities, housing facilities, social ties, and
   climate

Conditional Factors

Cost of move, distance,
economic status, family size,
liquidity of assets, sex,
education, occupational
skills, employment status,
and age

Socio-cultural System:
Values, beliefs, refer-
ence groups, etc.

Personal System:
Ambition, beliefs, status,
age, marital status, etc.

Communication System:
Formal and informal
sources

42

of residence, more adventuresome in taking risks to accept jobs in other areas, and more able to adjust to the new situation after moving.

The effect of unemployment on migration results in economic hardship which induces the unemployed person to seek and accept whatever job he can find wherever it is available.

Thus, migration for employment purposes is expected to be negatively related to age, positively related to education and occupational skills, and that the unemployed are more mobile than the employed.

If the above assumptions are correct, the variance between those who desire to move and those who do not will be explained in terms of perceived deprivation of one's wants in area of residence and perceived opportunities in area of destination to meet these wants. The variance between migrants and non-migrants will be explained in terms of any one or combination of the following factors, depending on the reason for moving: education, age, economic status, professional skills, marital status, family size, liquidity of assets, and sex.

This conceptualization of migration provides a comprehensive framework for much of what we know about migration theories and research; it places each of the factors involved in proper perspective and relates these factors to one another and to the various stages of the migration process in a systematic and meaningful way. Furthermore, all variables and assumptions are measurable and thus amenable to empirical verification. The model further allows for the possibility of adding and modifying variables.

Postulates and Hypotheses

The following postulates and hypotheses are derived from our earlier discussion in this chapter.

Postulate I

Given a more favorable balance in opportunity elsewhere, predisposition to move is positively related to felt deprivation of migrant's wants: employment opportunities, health facilities, education facilities, housing facilities, social relations, and climate.

Hypotheses

Assuming that the balance of opportunity favors another area:

1. Predisposition to migrate is positively related to felt deprivation of employment opportunities at area of residence.

2. Predisposition to migrate is positively related to felt deprivation of health facilities at area of residence.

3. Predisposition to migrate is positively related to felt deprivation of educational facilities at area of residence.

4. Predisposition to migrate is positively related to felt deprivation of social ties at area of residence.

5. Predisposition to migrate is positively related to felt deprivation of climate at area of residence.

Postulate II

Voluntary migration is a function of predisposition to move and economic status, family size, and liquidity of assets.

Hypotheses

6. Migration is positively related to predisposition to move.

Among those desiring to move:

7. Migration is negatively related to family size.

8. Migration is positively related to economic status.

9. Migration is negatively related to liquidity of assets.

Postulate III

Migration for employment reasons is selective of the educated, young adults, unemployed, males, and those with professional skills.

Hypotheses

When migration is for employment reasons:

10. Migration is positively related to education.

11. Migration is positively related to occupational skills.

12. Migration is inversely related to labor age.

13. Migration is more common among the unemployed than employed.

14. Migration is more common among males than females.

Footnotes

1. Goals, purposes, objectives, ends, reasons for moving, opportunities, wants, needs, desires are used interchangeably in migration studies.

2. See, for example, John K. Folger, "Models in Migration," Selected Studies of Migration Since World War II (New York, 1958), p. 159. In his discussion of migration models, Folger arrives at similar conclusions regarding the relationship between migration and other factors. He states: "In this conceptualization, the goals (of the migrant) are assumed to be the basic, underlying causes of migration. There are other factors which affect the migration process. These can be called limiting and facilitating conditions of migration. They are the situational factors which help determine when, where, and how much migration will take place."

3. Mangalam, op. cit., p. 9.

4. Runciman, op. cit., pp. 10-11.

5. These categories of factors were given by migrants as reasons for their move in studies conducted by John B. Lansing and Eva Mueller, The Geographic Mobility of Labor (Ann Arbor, 1967), pp. 36-39; Ronald L. Johnson and James R. Kiefert, "Factors Involved in the Decision to Migrate and the Impact of Migration Upon the Individual and the Sender and Receiver Community" (Unpublished Report, Grand Forks, North Dakota, 1968).

6. W. G. Runciman, Relative Deprivation and Social Justice: A Study of Attitudes to Social Inequality in Twentieth-Century England (Berkeley, 1966), p 21.

7. Ibid. Feasibility of having X was introduced by Runciman to distinguish it from a fantasy state of mind.

CHAPTER IV

RESEARCH DESIGN AND METHODOLOGY

This chapter will discuss the research design, study population and areas, data collection, design of analysis, and statistics used to test the theoretical model of migration outlined in Chapter V.

Research Design

Kerlinger notes that a "research design" has two basic purposes: (1) to provide answers to research questions and (2) to control covariance.[1] It will also be appropriate to add that the ultimate purpose of science and research design is to determine cause-effect relationships between phenomena under study.

There are two basic designs that social scientists use in their studies: (1) Experimental or before-after design, and (2) ex post facto or after-only design, sometimes referred to as nonexperimental design. The basic difference between the two designs is control and manipulation of the independent variable or variables and assignment of subjects or treatments to various experimental and control groups. In an experimental investigation, the investigator manipulates subjects physically and controls all other independent variables, then observes the dependent variable or variables for variation concomitant to the manipulation of the independent variable. In ex post facto research one cannot physically manipulate treatments or assign subjects, because in this kind of research design the independent variable or variables have already occurred. In this case, researcher starts with observation of the dependent variable and retrospectively attempts to determine the contributions of possible independent variables by statistical manipulation.[2]

Each of the above designs has advantages and disadvantages. We shall not dwell on this here, for there is a vast literature dealing with the subject. It is generally agreed, however, that in research to discover, classify, and measure phenomena and the factors behind such phenomena, the controlled experiment is the most desired model of science.[3]

Ex post facto design is used in this study. Thus, the effects of the independent variables, except for the hypothetical introduction of opportunities in destination area, are already present in the study population. Consequently, inferences about the relationship between the variables will be derived from the statistical manipulation of the data.

The Study Areas

The areas studied in this research involve seven rural postal routes - six postal routes in Campbell County and one in Clairborne County, Tennessee. Selection of these areas was determined by the East Tennessee Development District, the contracting agency for the present study.

Campbell County is located in the eastern part of the state on the Tennessee-Kentucky border. Its land area consists of 447 square miles of rugged, mostly mountainous terrain with over 75 percent of the land forested.

When studied, the population of Campbell County was 25,700, which is slightly less than its 1930 population of 26,827. A steady population loss has occurred since 1950 from 34,369 to 27,936 in 1960. This decline in population size is attributed in large part to migration due to greatly reduced mining operations upon which the major part of the county's economy is based. It is estimated that nearly one-third - 11,800 - of the county's population left Campbell County in the 1950-60 decade as jobs and opportunities disappeared.[4]

Campbell County is a rural, poverty-ridden area with four incorporated towns existing on a limited economic base. Forty-three percent of the 5,864 families now living in Campbell County are classified as poor. The Campbell County Welfare Department spends about four million dollars annually in the county. According to the Tennessee Department of Employment Security, the total labor force in the county is 6,640. Ten percent of these are unemployed, and about 20 percent are partly employed and/or underpaid.[5]

Although no statistics are available, the rural areas of the county had been the most dependent on, and were most affected by, the reduction in mining operations. The county's population loss was due mainly to rural people leaving the county. Poverty, unemployment, and dependence on welfare are more prevalent among the rural people than the urban population of the county.

The Study Population

A proportionate systematic random sample of 344 heads of household was drawn from seven rural postal routes in Campbell and Clairborne Counties. This consisted of drawing every fourth name from the list of names for each postal route, with the first name drawn randomly.

Lists of names of families residing in these areas, a total of 1,383 families, were obtained from the various local post offices. The total distribution of population and the various postal routes involved are shown in Table 2.

Out of the total sample, six persons could not be reached and five schedules were discarded for incomplete information, thus leaving a final sample of 333 heads of household.

TABLE 2

DISTRIBUTION OF FAMILIES BY AREA STUDIED

Rural Postal Route	County	Number of Families
Duff	Campbell	347
LaFollette	Campbell	230
Elk Valley	Campbell	247
Caryville	Campbell	95
Pioneer	Campbell	88
Morley	Campbell	57
Clairfield	Clairborne	319
Total Population		1383

Data Collection

Data were collected by means of an interview schedule which included both structured and open-ended questions (Appendix I). The entire schedule was pretested by the writer on fifteen persons before the final copy was constructed.

The interviewing team was made up of five graduate students from the University of Tennessee and four local persons from Campbell County. Prior to going into the field, all team members were given training until they were thoroughly familiar with the content of the schedule.

In order to avoid suspicion and to maximize cooperation by the respondents, the following steps were taken two weeks prior to the interview date to inform respondents about the purpose of the interview, the area to be covered, and to request their cooperation: (1) announcements were made over the local radio station; (2) articles accompanied by pictures of the interviewers were entered in the local newspaper; and (3) a post card, signed by the county agent, was sent to every respondent informing him when he would be interviewed and requesting his cooperation.

From the account of the interviewers afterward, all respondents were quite receptive and none refused to be interviewed.

Measurement of Variables and Index Construction

Felt Deprivation of Employment Opportunities - measured on five-point scale in terms of respondent's felt dissatisfaction with, and how good he feels about, the type of job he has and salary paid. [Appendix I, Q. 40(sum of b,c,p, and q).] Applies only to those who are eligible for work.

Felt Deprivation of Health Facilities - measured on five-point scale in terms of respondent's felt dissatisfaction with, and how good he feels about, doctors and hospitals in the area of residence. [Appendix I, Q. 40(sum of d,e,r, and s).]

Felt Deprivation of Educational Facilities - measured on five-point scale in terms of respondent's felt dissatisfaction with, and how good he feels about, schools and teachers in the area of residence. [Appendix I, Q. 40(f,g,t, and o).] Applies only to heads of family that have members of their family going to school.

Felt Deprivation of Housing Facilities - measured on five-point scale in terms of respondent's felt dissatisfaction with, and how good he feels about, his house, furnishings, and water supply. [Appendix I, Q. 40(sum of h,i,j,v, and w).]

Felt Deprivation of Social Ties - measured on five-point scale in terms of respondent's felt dissatisfaction with, and how good he feels about, his relationships with relatives, friends, and neighbors. [Appendix I, Q. 40(sum of k,l,m,x,y, and z).]

Felt Deprivation of Climate - measured on five-point scale in terms of respondent's felt dissatisfaction with, and how good he feels about, the local weather and climate. [Appendix I, Q. 40(sum of n and z_1).

For each of the six indexes mentioned above, all questionnaire items that pertain to aspects of predisposition to migrate are used.

Perceived Opportunities in Area of Destination and Predisposition to Move - combined and measured on three-point scale in terms of predisposition to move for better:

1. Employment Opportunities. (Appendix I, Q. 30c).

2. Health Facilities. (Appendix I, Q. 27c).

3. Educational Facilities. (Appendix I, Q. 28c).

4. Housing Facilities. (Appendix I, Q. 29c).

5. Social Ties. (Appendix I, Q. 32c).

6. Climate. (Appendix I, Q. 31c).

7. All of the above. (Appendix I, Q. 33).

Sex: Male vs. female. (Appendix I, Q. 2).

Marital Status: Single vs. married. (Appendix I, Q. 3).

Age - grouped into nine categories from below age 19 to over age 75. (Appendix I, Q. 4).

Education - grouped into nine categories from no education to postgraduate. (Appendix I, Q. 5).

Employment Status: Employed vs. unemployed. (Appendix I, Q. 6).

Professional Skills - measured in terms of number of jobs held by the respondent. (Appendix I, Q. 7b).

Fixed Assets - measured in terms of house ownership. (Appendix I, Q. 11).

Family Size - measured in terms of number of people living in the same house. (Appendix I, Q. 13).

Economic Status - measured in terms of the family's total annual income, and grouped into seventeen categories. (Appendix I, Q. 59).

Plans to Move - measured on three-point scale in terms of respondent's plans to move in the near future. (Appendix I, Q. 22).

General Migration - refers to those desiring to move for any reason or reasons. Measured on three-point scale. (Appendix I, Q. 33).

Migration for Employment Purposes - refers to those desiring to move for better employment opportunities only. Measured on three-point scale. (Appendix I, Q. 30c).

Design of Analysis

Seltiz's type of evidence, Blalock's recursive system, and Lazarsfeld's multivariate analysis is used in this study to analyze and make causal inferences from non-experimental data. A brief discussion of these approaches is presented below.

Seltiz outlines three types of evidence in testing hypotheses about causal relationships between the independent and dependent variables. These types of evidence are:

1. Evidence of concomitant variation, that is X and Y - the independent and dependent variables - is associated in the way predicted by the hypothesis.

2. Evidence of time order of occurrence of variables, that is, Y did not occur before X.

3. Evidence ruling out other factors as possible determining conditions of Y.[6]

The recursive system advanced by Blalock assumes one-way causation. For example, if a particular X_i is taken as a cause of X_j, then X_j cannot cause X_i. There is no single dependent or independent variable in a recursive system. The system involves an initial variable, labeled an exogenous variable, that is caused by unknown factors outside the system. Using this exogenous variable as a starting point, the variables that follow sequentially may be dependent or independent. For example, in a hypothetical model of simple causal chain involving four variables,

$(X_1 \rightarrow X_2 \rightarrow X_3 \rightarrow X_4)$, X_1 is taken to be independent of all the rest. Its value is determined only by variables that are outside the causal system. X_2, on the other hand, depends on both X_1 and the outside variables as well. In turn, X_3 depends on X_1, X_2, and outside variables. Finally, X_4 depends on all other variables: X_1, X_2, X_3, and outside variables.[7]

According to the recursive system rationale, testing the validity of specific causal models requires the satisfaction of three criteria: (1) the largest correlations should occur between variables adjacent in the system; (2) partial correlations should approximate zero when intervening factors are held constant, and (3) X_1 is prior in time to X_2, X_2 is prior in time to X_3, etc. In terms of the hypothetical model used above, the size of the correlations between the four variables will be as follows: (r_{12}), (r_{23}), and (r_{34}) (r_{13}) and (r_{24}) (r_{14}). Furthermore, $r_{14} = (r_{12})(r_{23})(r_{34})$, indicating that the correlation between X_1 and X_4 is weaker than any of the correlations between intermediate variables.

As far as the partials are concerned, all partials $(r_{13.2})$, $(r_{24.3})$ and $(r_{14.23})$ should approximate zero. In case of the latter equation $(r_{14.23})$, if there is a simple causal chain $X_1 \rightarrow X_2 \rightarrow X_3 \rightarrow X_4$, the partial between X_1 and X_4 will disappear if either of the intervening variables X_2 or X_3 is controlled.[8]

Lazarsfeld's approach for making inferences about causal relationships between variables is similar but not the same as Blalock's recursive system and Seltiz's types of evidence. He distinguishes between four types of elaborations, Figure 2. The assumptions here are that if we start out with a relation between two variables, X and Y, with X being prior to Y in the time sequence, then the test variable, t, is introduced. If the relationship between X and Y does not disappear for any antecedent test factor, then the original relationship should be called a causal one. If, on the other hand, the partial relationship between X and Y changes or disappears upon the introduction of a test factor, then we will have one of four types of elaborations:

FIGURE 2

TYPES OF ELABORATIONS

	I	II
	$[xt] = 0$	$[xt] \neq 0$
Position of t	$[xy;t] \neq 0$	$[xy;t] = 0$
Antecedent (or simultaneous with X)	PA	MA
Intervening	PI	MI

PA (condition), PI (contingency), MA (Spurious), or MI (interpretation).

52

In PA and PI types, the original correlation changes, and one of the two new partials is larger than the original relationship. Furthermore, if "t" is a condition (types PA), then "x" is a contingency. If "t" is a contingency (type PI), then "x" is a condition.

In MA and MI types, the original correlation approximates zero, and the two newly emerging relationships are always larger than the original.[9]

Statistics

In choosing among alternative statistical tests to analyze data, one should select the test that meets the following characteristics:

1. A test whose assumptions are met by the data.

2. The most powerful test, that is, the test that uses more information and is more likely to reject the null hypothesis when it is false.

3. A test that handles the most number of variables under study and measures the degree of association between them.

To test the size of relationship or level of significance between variables, a number of parametric and non-parametric statistical tests are available. Parametric tests, however, have more stringent assumptions for their application as compared with non-parametric tests. Accordingly, one may use, at the risk of losing power, non-parametric tests under parametric test conditions, but not vice versa. Furthermore, results of non-parametric tests have wider application in sociology.

The parametric statistical model assumes the following conditions:

1. The observations must be independent (this assumption underlies non-parametric statistics as well).

2. The observations must be drawn from normally distributed populations.

3. These populations must have the same variance.

4. The variables involved must have been measured on at least an interval scale (this is not shared by all parametric statistical tests).

For analysis of variance (F test), another condition is added:

5. The means of these normal and homoscedastic populations must be linear combinations of effects. That is, the effects must be additive.

With the exception of condition four (4) and possibly condition five (5), these conditions are ordinarily not tested in the course of the performance of a statistical analysis. Rather, they are assumptions.[10]

Since we will not be dealing with F test in the study, the only criterion to be considered for choosing between a parametric and non-parametric test will be the level of measurement.

The variables involved in the present study have been measured on different scales: interval, ordinal, and nominal.

Interval Scale: age, education, income, and occupational skills.

Ordinal Scale: dissatisfaction with employment opportunities, educational facilities, health facilities, housing facilities, social ties, and climate; predisposition to move; and plans to migrate.

Nominal Scale: marital status, liquidity of assets, sex, and employment status.

In our case, data analysis involves measuring the degree of association between interval and ordinal, ordinal and ordinal, and ordinal and nominal scales. Some appropriate statistical tests to measure these associations are listed below.

1. Test for Describing Association between one Nominal and one Ordinal Scale: coefficient of differentiation, 0 (theta).[11]

2. Tests for Describing Associations between Ordinal Scales and between Ordinal and Interval Scales: (1) Kendall rank correlation coefficient[12] (non-parametric) and (2) Pearson product moment correlation[13] (parametric).

If we have evidence to believe that parametric conditions - normal distribution of population and equal variance - are met in our data under analysis, then one should choose the Pearson product moment correlation over Kendall rank correlation because it is a more powerful test, that is, more likely to reject the null hypothesis when false. Since we do not know the population distribution nor its variance and their possible effects on r's results, the present data were analyzed by both tests. The results showed some inconsistency between the two tests, presumably due to lack of normal distribution and the homoscedasticity of the sub-samples. Consequently, Kendall's rank correlation should be chosen. But, because multiple and partial correlation will be needed for certain equations, a function that Kendall coefficient cannot perform, Pearson's product moment correlation is used in this aspect of the analysis.

Footnotes

1. Fred N. Kerlinger, <u>Foundations of Behavioral Research: Educational and Psychological Inquiry</u> (New York, 1964), p. 275.

2. For excellent references and detailed discussion on this subject consult Kerlinger, <u>op. cit.</u>, pp. 275-320; William J. Goode and Paul K. Hatt, <u>Methods in Social Research</u> (New York, 1952), pp. 74-90.

3. Kerlinger, <u>op. cit.</u>, p. 291.

4. East Tennessee Development District, "Campbell County Demonstration Project: A Comprehensive Plan" (Unpublished Report, East Tennessee Development District, 1969).

5. <u>Ibid</u>.

6. Claire Seltiz and others, <u>Research Methods in Social Relations</u>, ren. ed. (Washington, D.C., 1963), pp. 83-88.

7. Hubert M. Blalock, <u>Causal Inferences in Nonexperimental Research</u> (Chapel Hill, North Carolina, 1964), p. 54.

8. <u>Ibid</u>., pp. 62-70.

9. Paul F. Lazarsfeld, "Interpretation of Statistical Relations as a Research Operation," <u>The Language of Social Research</u>, Paul F. Lazarsfeld and Morris Rosenberg, eds. (Glencoe, 1955), pp. 115-25.

10. Sidney Siegel, <u>Nonparametric Statistics for the Behavioral Sciences</u> (New York, 1956), p. 19.

11. Linton C. Freeman, <u>Elementary Applied Statistics: For Students of Behavioral Science</u> (New York, 1965), p. 108.

12. Siegel, <u>op. cit.</u>, pp. 213-23.

13. Quin McNemar, <u>Psychological Statistics</u>, 3rd ed. (New York, 1962), pp. 112-275.

CHAPTER V

DEPRIVATION, PREDISPOSITION TO MOVE, AND PLANS TO MIGRATE

The purpose of this chapter is to test the validity of the migration model discussed in the preceding chapter. More specifically, it will seek to verify the following hypotheses:

1. Existence of migration stages: deprivation, predisposition to move, and plans to migrate.

2. Effects of deprivation of employment opportunities, educational facilities, health facilities, housing facilities, social ties, and climate on predisposition to move.

3. Effects of predisposition to move, economic status, family size, liquidity of assets, sex, education, occupational skills, age, and employment status on plans to migrate.

The strategy of data analysis involves consideration of two consecutive and separate stages: conditions leading to predisposition to move and conditions leading to plans to migrate. The first stage of analysis involves the entire population or sample. The second involves only those who are predisposed to move. The reason for selection of the latter subgroup is because we are interested in determining why people desiring to move do not plan to migrate. Since, as it will be demonstrated later on, none of those not predisposed to move had plans to migrate, it is not appropriate to include them in the analysis. Excluding from the analysis those who are not predisposed to move is equivalent to holding constant the effects of deprivation in area of residence and availability of opportunities in area of destination on predisposition to move, which are analyzed in the first step.

Figure 3 depicts the various assumptions and factors contained in the theoretical model and the hypotheses to be tested. As a first step, we shall examine the existence of the three migration stages and determine the time order between them.

FIGURE 3

RESEARCH MODEL DEPICTING STAGES AND FACTORS INVOLVED IN VOLUNTARY MIGRATION

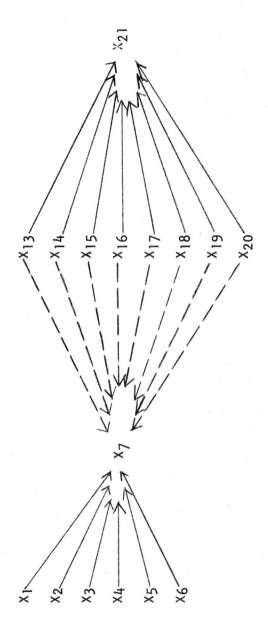

X1:   deprivation of employment opportunities.
X2:   deprivation of educational facilities.
X3:   deprivation of health facilities.
X4:   deprivation of housing facilities.
X5:   deprivation of social ties.
X6:   deprivation of climate.
X7:   predisposition to move.
X13: economic status.

X14: family size.
X15: liquidity of assets.
X16: education.
X17: occupational skills.
X18: age.
X19: employment status.
X20: sex.
X21: plans to move.

Existence of the Three Stages of Migration:
Deprivation, Predisposition to Move,
and Plans to Migrate

Statistical manipulation of the independent and dependent variables can never establish a time order between them. The size of a correlation between two variables is not affected by choice of one as independent (or dependent). However, if there is a chain of causation, as in a recursive system, the relationships between the adjacent variables must be greater than those farther away. Furthermore, the relationships between the distant factors in the chain of causation should approximate zero when any of the factors lying in between them is controlled.

According to our theoretical model, the following chain of causation is assumed: deprivation——→predisposition to move——→plans to migrate. If this model is valid, then the following relationships should hold:

1.   Predisposition to move must be significantly related to both deprivation and plans to migrate.

2.   The relationship between deprivation and predisposition to move should be stronger than that between deprivation and plans to migrate. In like manner, the relationship between predisposition to move and plans to migrate should be greater than that between deprivation and plans to migrate.

3.   The partial relationship between deprivation and plans to migrate should approximate zero if we control for predisposition to move.

4.   Time order, that is, deprivation precedes predisposition to move and predisposition to move precedes plans to migrate.

The above statistical relationships between deprivation, predisposition to move, and plans to migrate establish only one condition of the chain of causation predicted in the migration model: <u>predisposition to move is situated in between deprivation and plans to migrate</u>. The statistical analysis, however, cannot distinguish between the following alternative chains of causation: deprivation——→predisposition to move——→ plans to migrate and the situation in which all arrows are reversed, that is, plans to migrate——→predisposition to move——→deprivation, or this: deprivation←—— predisposition to move——→ plans to migrate. However, some insight is gained through tabular analysis.

Tabular Analysis

A two-way frequency distribution between predisposition to move and "assumed" opportunities at the area of destination is shown in Table 3. Sixty-two percent of the sample population indicated they would like to move, if they could, to another area that has better jobs, better doctors and hospitals, better teachers and schools, and nicer home and furnishings, and cleaner neighborhood than their area of residence. On the other hand, only one percent will be willing to move to another area that is not better on these characteristics than is their place of residence. Thus, assuming that the "assumed" availability of opportunities elsewhere is an indicator of deprivation of these opportunities - employment, education facilities, health facilities, housing facilities, social ties, and climate, and that deprivation precedes (in time) predisposition to move, then deprivation is a necessary but not sufficient condition for predisposition to move.

TABLE 3

DISTRIBUTION OF RESPONDENTS BY PREDISPOSITION TO MOVE AND OPPORTUNITIES AT THE AREA OF DESTINATION

		Predisposition to Move		
		No, Do Not Know	Yes	Total
Better Opportunities at Area of Destination	No Opportunities Are Available	329	4	333
		(99%)	(1%)	(100%)
	Opportunities Are Available	124	209	333
		(38%	(62%)	(100%)

*The original question was whether respondents would like to move to another place having better job opportunities, educational facilities, health facilities, housing, relatives, and climate. Two hundred nine respondents answered positively while 124 said they would not move or did not know. Then the 209 respondents predisposed to move were sorted out on whether they would move to another place that is no better off than their area of residence. Only four respondents remained in the "Yes" category while all others, 229, ended up in the "No" and "Don't Know" category.

Table 4 depicts the relationship between predisposition to move and plans to migrate. Twenty-one percent of those desiring to move had plans to migrate, while none of those not predisposed to move had any plans to migrate. If we assume on theoretical grounds that predisposition to move precedes plans to move, the analysis indicates that predisposition to move is a necessary but not sufficient condition for plans to migrate.

TABLE 4

DISTRIBUTION OF RESPONDENTS BY PLANS TO MIGRATE AND
PREDISPOSITION TO MOVE FOR BETTER: EMPLOYMENT
OPPORTUNITIES, HEALTH FACILITIES, EDUCATIONAL
FACILITIES, HOUSING, SOCIAL TIES, AND CLIMATE

		Plans to Move	
		No, Do Not Know	Yes
Predisposition to Move	No, Do Not Know	124 (100%)	0 (0%)
	Yes	178 (85%)	31 (15%)

It may be concluded from the above tabular analysis that: (1) the three stages of migration - deprivation, predisposition to move, and plans to migrate - exist, (2) deprivation is a necessary but not sufficient condition for predisposition to move, and predisposition to move is a necessary but not sufficient condition for plans to migrate, if one is willing to assume on theoretical grounds an order of occurrence of these phenomena. The analysis, however, does not prove the causal relationship between the migration stages nor the hypothesized time order between them, for it is possible that all three may occur at the same time.

The causal relationship between deprivation of specific factors, predisposition to move, and plans to migrate as well as the time sequence between them are examined below.

60

Recursive System Analysis

Deprivation of Employment Opportunities, Predisposition to Move and Plans to Migrate

Figure 4 shows the zero order correlation and partial correlation coefficients between deprivation of employment opportunities (X_1), predisposition to move (X_7), and plans to migrate (X_{21}).

1. Predisposition to move (X_7) is significantly related to both deprivation of employment opportunities (X_1) in area of residence and to plans to migrate (X_{21}), with zero order correlations of .52 and .21, respectively.

2. The zero order correlation coefficient of .13 between deprivation of employment opportunities and plans to migrate is smaller than either of the correlations involving predisposition to move for better employment opportunities and the other two variables.

3. The relationship between deprivation of employment opportunities and plans to migrate is significantly reduced to .02 when predisposition to move for better employment opportunities is held constant.

Since all relationships are in the predicted direction and since as shown for the general case deprivation may precede predisposition to move, and the latter precede plans to migrate, it may be concluded that the three stages of deprivation of employment opportunities, predisposition to move, and plans to migrate exist, and the presumption of the time sequence assumed in the model is increased. That is, deprivation of employment opportunities leads to predisposition to move and eventually to plans to migrate.

Deprivation of Educational Facilities, Predisposition to Move and Plans to Migrate

Figure 5 indicates:

1. Predisposition to move (X_7) is significantly related to both deprivation of educational facilities (X_2) and plans to migrate (X_{21}) with zero order correlation coefficients of .78 and .18, respectively.

2. The zero order correlation coefficient of .22 between deprivation of educational facilities and plans to migrate is smaller than that of .78 between deprivation of educational facilities and predisposition to move, but slightly larger than .18 between predisposition to move and plans to migrate.

FIGURE 4

PRODUCT MOMENT ZERO ORDER AND PARTIAL CORRELATIONS BETWEEN DEPRIVATION OF EMPLOYMENT OPPORTUNITIES (X_1), PREDISPOSITION TO MOVE (X_7), AND PLANS TO MOVE (X_{21})*

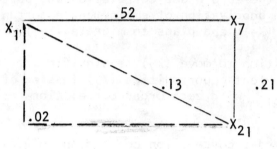

$r_{1,21.07}$

*Solid lines indicate theoretically predicted relationships in all figures throughout the remainder of this text.

3. The relationship between deprivation of educational facilities and plans to migrate is reduced to .13 after controlling for predisposition to move.

In general, the data do not fit the relationships assumed in the recursive system, for the correlation of .18 between predisposition to move for better educational facilities and plans to migrate is smaller than that between deprivation of educational facilities and plans to migrate (r = .22).

The result may lead one to change the path sequence hypothesized in Figure 5 to: predisposition to move———>deprivation———>plans to migrate. This alternative path assumes that predisposition to move is prior to deprivation. Another possible alternative is that deprivation of educational facilities has a direct influence on both predisposition to move and plans to migrate. The partial correlation between predisposition to move and plans to migrate, with deprivation of educational facilities controlled, is (.07), which suggests that one or the other of these alternative hypotheses is superior to the initial hypothesis.

It may be concluded from the data analysis that predisposition to move by itself does not induce people to make plans to migrate. However, whether predisposition to move is a consequence or cause of deprivation in educational opportunities depends on evidence of the time priority of these two variables. As this is not available, a choice of the most probable of these alternative hypotheses cannot be made.

FIGURE 5

PRODUCT MOMENT ZERO ORDER AND PARTIAL CORRELATIONS
BETWEEN DEPRIVATION OF EDUCATIONAL FACILITIES (X_2),
PREDISPOSITION TO MOVE (X_7) AND
PLANS TO MIGRATE (X_{21})

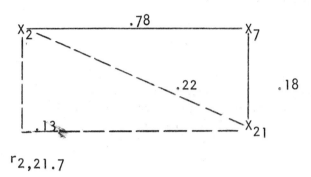

$r_{2,21.7}$

Deprivation of Health Facilities, Predisposition to Move and Plans to Migrate

The relationships among these factors are presented in Figure 6 and indicate:

1. Predisposition to move (X_7) is significantly related to deprivation of health facilities (X_3) and to plans to migrate (X_{21}) with zero order correlation coefficients of .29 and .30, respectively.

2. The zero order correlation coefficient of .36 between deprivation of health facilities and plans to migrate is larger than either of the other two relationships.

3. The original relationship of .36 between deprivation of health facilities and plans to move is slightly and insignificantly reduced to .30 after controlling for predisposition to move.

The statistical relationships between deprivation of health facilities, predisposition to move, and plans to migrate do not correspond to the tenets of the recursive model of chain of causation explained earlier. That is, the relationship of .36 between deprivation of health facilities and plans to migrate is not smaller than either between predisposition to move and deprivation or between predisposition to move and plans to migrate. Furthermore, the partial correlation between deprivation of health facilities and plans to migrate remains relatively high (.30) after controlling for predisposition to move. In like manner, the relationship between predisposition to move for better health facilities and plans to migrate, after controlling for deprivation of health facilities, drops only slightly to .23 (Figure 6). Thus, the theoretical assumptions about the time order between deprivation of health facilities, predisposition to move and plans to migrate are invalid. However, this does not rule out the possibility that they are causally related in some way, since the partial coefficient between them does not approach zero and remains significant and moderately high.

FIGURE 6

PRODUCT MOMENT ZERO ORDER AND PARTIAL CORRELATIONS
BETWEEN DEPRIVATION OF HEALTH FACILITIES (X_3),
PREDISPOSITION TO MOVE FOR BETTER
HEALTH FACILITIES (X_9), AND
PLANS TO MOVE (X_{21})

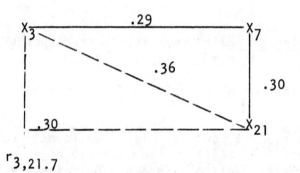

$r_{3,21.7}$

Deprivation of Housing Facilities, Predisposition to
Move, and Plans to Migrate

The relationships between deprivation of housing facilities (X_3), predisposition to move (X_7), and plans to migrate (X_{21}) are shown in Figure 7.

1. Predisposition to move is significantly related to deprivation of housing facilities and to plans to migrate with zero order correlation coefficients of .41 and .33, respectively.

2.   The zero order correlation coefficient of .28 between deprivation of housing facilities and plans to migrate is smaller than either of the other zero order relationships.

3.   The original relationship of .28 between deprivation of housing facilities and plans to migrate is significantly reduced to .17, although not to zero, after controlling for predisposition to move.

All the above relationships are in the predicted direction. Evidently, deprivation of housing facilities contributes in some degree to predisposition to move and then to the development of plans to migrate.

FIGURE 7

PRODUCT MOMENT ZERO ORDER AND PARTIAL CORRELATIONS
BETWEEN DEPRIVATION OF HOUSING FACILITIES (X_4)
PREDISPOSITION TO MOVE (X_7), AND
PLANS TO MIGRATE (X_{21})

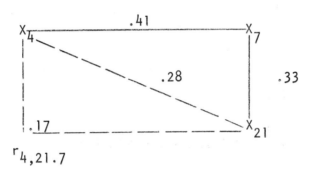

Deprivation of Social Ties, Predisposition to Move,
and Plans to Migrate

Figure 8 depicts the correlations between these factors.

1.   Predisposition to move (X_7) is significantly related to deprivation of social ties (X_5) and plans to migrate (X_{21}) with zero order correlation coefficients of .17 and .33, respectively.

2.   The zero order correlation coefficient of .13 between deprivation of social ties and plans to migrate is smaller than the correlationships of .17 between deprivation of social ties and predisposition to move, and .33 between predisposition to move and plans to migrate.

3. The original relationship of .13 between deprivation of social ties and plans to migrate approximates zero (r=.07) after controlling for predisposition to move.

All of the above relationships are in the predicted direction. Thus, the theoretical assumptions of the model about the existence of and time order between deprivation of social ties, predisposition to move, and plans to migrate are plausible in this case.

FIGURE 8

PRODUCT MOMENT ZERO ORDER AND PARTIAL CORRELATIONS
BETWEEN DEPRIVATION OF SOCIAL TIES (X_5), PREDISPOSITION
TO MOVE (X_7), AND PLANS TO MIGRATE (X_{21})

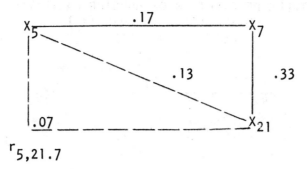

Deprivation of Climate, Predisposition to Move, and Plans to Migrate

The correlations between these factors are outlined in Figure 9.

1. Predisposition to move (X_7) is significantly related to both deprivation of climate (X_6) in the area of residence and plans to migrate (X_{21}), with zero order correlations of .41 and .27, respectively.

2. The zero order relationship of .27 between deprivation of climate and plans to migrate is smaller than the relationship between deprivation of climate and predisposition to move, but the same size as the correlation between predisposition to move and plans to migrate.

3. The original relationship of .27 between deprivation of climate at area of destination and plans to migrate is reduced to .19 after controlling for predisposition to move.

66

The relationships are in the predicted direction, but not sufficient to provide strong support for the proposed model. The data support equally well the alternative model: predisposition to move for better climate ——→ deprivation of climate ——→ plans to migrate. The time order of deprivation and predisposition to move is once again the crucial factor on which to reject one of the alternatives. Unfortunately, time order is not determined. Thus, the data do not help us eliminate one of the models as invalid.

Three conclusions may be drawn from the above tabular and recursive system analyses:

1. Deprivation of employment opportunities, housing facilities, and social ties may contribute directly to development of predisposition to move and indirectly to making plans to migrate in the following time sequence: deprivation ——→ predisposition to move ——→ plans to migrate. However, a strong presumption of this model is provided only for employment opportunities.

2. For educational facilities the data do not support the proposed model, but support two alternative hypotheses equally well, namely, either: (a) deprivation causes predisposition to move and plans to migrate, but predisposition does not lead to plans to migrate, or (b) predisposition to move stimulates deprivation, which leads to plans to move. The crucial factor in choice of these alternative hypotheses is the time order of deprivation and predisposition to move. As this information is not available, an inference as to the most probable model cannot be made.

3. The assumed chain of causation and time order between deprivation of health facilities, predisposition to move, and plans to migrate is invalid.

FIGURE 9

PRODUCT MOMENT ZERO ORDER AND PARTIAL CORRELATIONS BETWEEN DEPRIVATION OF CLIMATE (X_6), PREDISPOSITION TO MOVE (X_7), AND PLANS TO MIGRATE (X_{21})

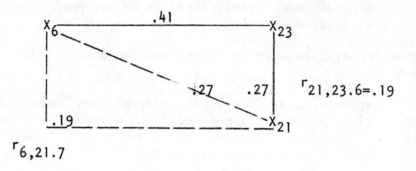

Effects of Deprivation of Employment Opportunities, Educational Facilities, Health Facilities, Housing Facilities, Social Ties, and Climate
on Predisposition to Move

Attempts will be made here to measure the degree of relationship, if there is any, between predisposition to move and each of deprivation of employment opportunities, educational facilities, health facilities, housing facilities, social ties, and climate.

As indicated earlier in the Methodology Chapter, three types of evidence are required to establishing causation between two variables. They are: (1) concomitant variation, (2) time order, and (3) ruling out the effects of other confounding factors. We have developed a presumption of a time order between deprivation and predisposition to move in the general case and for certain, but not all, types of deprivation, separately. Now we shall proceed to examine the other two types of evidence: concomitant variation and controlling the effects of other confounding factors under consideration. Thus, if these types of evidence are present, then our confidence in the relationship between deprivation and predisposition to move is strengthened.

An examination of Table 5 indicates that there are significant relationships among the six independent factors - deprivation of employment opportunities (X_1), educational facilities (X_2), health facilities (X_3), housing facilities (X_4), social ties (X_5), and climate (X_6) - as well as between them and the dependent variable, predisposition to move. In order to determine the importance of each factor and its independent and interdependent contribution to the dependent variable, it will be necessary to use multiple and partial correlation. Interpretation of these coefficients is discussed below.

A simple correlation coefficient, such as r_{12}, indicates that the differences in variable (X_1) is considered as due to, or associated with, the difference in variable (X_2). This apparent relationship, however, may be spurious in that it may be due to the influence of other factor(s) that may be operating on variable (X_1), variable (X_2), or both. In many types of problems, such as our present study, the differences in one variable may be due to a number of other variables, all acting at the same time. In such a case, it will be desirable and useful to use multiple and partial correlation to measure and determine the importance of the joint and separate effects of the other variables under consideration. Multiple correlation coefficient, such as $r_{1.234}$, measures the combined importance or effects of factors (X_2), (X_3), and (X_4) as means of explaining the differences in the dependent factor (X_1). Partial correlation coefficient on the other hand, such as $r_{12.345}$, measures the correlation between the dependent factor (X_1) and the independent factor (X_2), while eliminating any tendency of the remaining independent factors $(X_3, X_4, \text{and } X_5)$ to obscure the relation. The coefficient of partial correlation is defined as a measure of the extent to which that part of the variation in the dependent variable which was not explained by the other independent factors can be explained by the addition of the new factor; while the coefficient of multiple correlation may be defined as the simple correlation between the actual values of the dependent variable and the values estimated from the several independent factors.

TABLE 5

MATRIX OF ZERO ORDER KENDALL RANK CORRELATION COEFFICIENT FOR TWELVE VARIABLES*

Variables	X_1	X_2	X_3	X_4	X_5	X_6	X_7	X_8	X_9	X_{10}	X_{11}	X_{12}
X_1 Deprivation of Employment Opportunities		.27	.12	.07	.05	.06	.53	.29	-.11	-.02	-.06	-.03
X_2 Deprivation of Education Facilities			.13	.17	.23	.04	.40	.75	.12	.16	.16	.02
X_3 Deprivation of Health Facilities				.44	.26	.35	.14	.04	.21	.25	.18	.26
X_4 Deprivation of Housing Facilities					.32	.34	.09	.09	.23	.32	.26	.17
X_5 Deprivation of Social Ties						.08	.05	.11	**	.20	.16	.09
X_6 Deprivation of Climate							.06	-.06	**	.19	.24	.33
X_7 Predisposition to Move for Better Employment Facilities								.46	.13	.21	.09	.07
X_8 Predisposition to Move for Better Education Facilities									.10	.17	.13	.01

Variables	X_1	X_2	X_3	X_4	X_5	X_6	X_7	X_8	X_9	X_{10}	X_{11i}	X_{12}
X_9 Predisposition to Move for Better Health Facilities										.43	.42	.42
X_{10} Predisposition to Move for Better Housing Facilities											.40	.37
X_{11} Predisposition to Move for Better Social Ties												.41
X_{12} Predisposition to Move for Better Climate												

* Sample size: 333; those that do not apply are ignored.

**Missing data.

71

Effects of Deprivation of Employment Opportunities on Predisposition to Move for Better Employment Opportunities

Hypothesis 1

Assuming better employment opportunities at the area of destination, predisposition to move is positively related to deprivation of employment opportunities at the area of residence.

A significant positive relationship (r = .38; tau = .50) was obtained between predisposition to move for better employment opportunities (X_7) and deprivation of employment opportunities (X_1) (Table 6).

TABLE 6

RELATIONSHIP BETWEEN DEPRIVATION OF EMPLOYMENT
OPPORTUNITIES (X_1) AND PREDISPOSITION TO MOVE
FOR BETTER EMPLOYMENT OPPORTUNITIES (X_7)

Measure of Relationship	Strength of Relationship	Level of Significance
Pearson $r_{7,1}$	.38*	.05
Kendall tau 7,1	.50**	.05
$R_{7.1,2,3,4,5,6}$	.46*	.05
$R^2_{7.1,2,3,4,5,6}$	.21*	
$r_{7,1.2,3,4,5,6}$	.18*	.05
$r^2_{7,1.2,3,4,5,6}$	.03*	

* Sample size: 118.

**Sample size: 333; those that do not apply are ignored.

Introducing the other five independent variables - deprivation of education facilities (X_2), health facilities (X_3), housing facilities (X_4), social ties (X_5), and climate (X_6) - into the equation increased the magnitude of correlation slightly from r = .38 to R = .46. When the effects of these five variables were partialled out, the correlation coefficient dropped to .18.

The partial correlation is in the predicted direction and significant at the .05 level, which lend support to the hypothesis. That is, predisposition to move is positively and causally related to deprivation of employment opportunities at the area of residence. However, the separate contribution of deprivation of employment opportunities to predisposition to move is very small, 3 percent of the total variance.

Effects of Deprivation of Educational Facilities On
Predisposition to Move for Better Educational Opportunities

Hypothesis 2

Assuming better educational facilities at the destination area, predisposition to move is positively related to deprivation of educational facilities at area of residence.

It can be observed in Table 7 that predisposition to move for better educational facilities (X_8) is strongly and positively related to deprivation of educational facilities (X_2) (r = .47; tau = .76). Although there is a substantial difference in the two measures of the relationship, Pearson's r is a more conservative estimate of the degree of a relationship between the variables.

The total effects of the six independent variables on predisposition to move for better educational facilities give a multiple correlation of .50 which is not significantly larger than the simple correlation of .47. Likewise, partialling out the effects of the five additional factors reduce the relationship between predisposition to move and deprivation of educational facilities to .37, which again is not a significant reduction.

Since all the relationships are highly significant and in the predicted direction, the hypothesis is strongly upheld. That is, predisposition to move is positively and causally related to deprivation of educational facilities at the area of residence, with the latter contributing 14 per cent of the total variance of predisposition to move.

TABLE 7

RELATIONSHIP BETWEEN DEPRIVATION OF EDUCATIONAL FACILITIES (X_2)
AND PREDISPOSITION TO MOVE FOR BETTER EDUCATIONAL
FACILITIES (X_8)

Measure of Relationship	Strength of Relationship	Level of Significance
Pearson $r_{8,2}$	.47*	.05
Kendall tau 8,2	.76**	.05
$R_{8.1,2,3,4,5,6}$	.50*	.05
$R^2_{8.1,2,3,4,5,6}$	.25*	
$r_{8,2.1,3,4,5,6}$	.37*	.05
$r^2_{8,2.1,3,4,5,6}$	.14*	

* Sample size: 118.
**Sample size: 333; those that do not apply are ignored.

Effects of Deprivation of Health Facilities on
Predisposition to Move for Better Health Facilities

Hypothesis 3

Assuming better health facilities at area of destination, predisposition to move is positively related to deprivation of health facilities at area of residence.

Data in Table 8 lend support to the hypothesized relationships. It can be seen in Table 8 that a positive and significant zero order correlationship ($r = .26$; tau = .21 for the subsample of 118) exists between deprivation of health facilities (X_3) and predisposition to move for better health facilities (X_9). A moderate multiple correlation of .31 is contributed by all six independent factors, thus contributing very little, .05, to the original zero order correlation coefficient. In like manner, the relationship between predisposition to move for better health facilities (X_9) and deprivation of health facilities (X_3), with the other five fariables held constant, was reduced slightly to .21, again a difference of .05 from the zero order correlation coefficient of .26.

74

Although the simple and partial correlations varied from weak to moderate, all were significant at the 5 per cent level and in the predicted direction; thus supporting the hypothesis. That is, predisposition to move is positively and causally related to deprivation of health facilities, with the latter contributing an average of 4 per cent to the total variance of predisposition to move.

TABLE 8

RELATIONSHIP BETWEEN DEPRIVATION OF HEALTH FACILITIES
(X_3) AND PREDISPOSITION TO MOVE FOR BETTER
HEALTH FACILITIES (X_9)

Measure of Relationship	Strength of Relationship	Level of Significance
Pearson $r_{9,3}$	.26*	.05
Kendall tau 9,3	.21**	
$R_{9.1,2,3,4,5,6}$	.31*	.05
$R^2_{9.1,2,3,4,5,6}$	.10*	
$r_{9,3.1,2,4,5,6}$	.21*	.05
$r^2_{9,3.1,2,4,5,6}$	.04*	

* Sample size: 118.

**Sample size: 333.

Effects of Deprivation of Housing Facilities on Predisposition to Move for Better Housing Facilities

Hypothesis 4

Assuming better housing facilities at the area of destination, predisposition to move is positively related to deprivation of housing facilities at area of residence.

The simple, multiple, and partial association between predisposition to move for better housing facilities (X_{10}) and deprivation of housing facilities (X_4) is shown in Table 9. The zero order correlation coefficients (r = .31) between the two variables is significant at the 5 per cent level and is in the hypothesized direction. Likewise, the multiple correlations of .41 are also significant.

TABLE 9

RELATIONSHIP BETWEEN DEPRIVATION OF HOUSING FACILITIES (X_4) AND PREDISPOSITION TO MOVE FOR BETTER HOUSING FACILITIES (X_{10})

Measure of Relationship	Strength of Relationship	Level of Significance
Pearson $r_{10,4}$	.31*	.05
Kendall tau 10,4	.32**	.05
$R_{10.1,2,3,4,5,6}$	.41*	.05
$R^2_{10.1,2,3,4,5,6}$	.17*	
$r_{10,4.1,2,3,5,6}$	.09*	.05
$r^2_{10,4.1,2,3,5,6}$	.01*	

* Sample size: 118.

**Sample size: 333.

Regarding the partial relationships, Table 9 reveals that a very weak and insignificant partial r = .09 between predisposition to migrate for better housing facilities and deprivation of housing facilities is obtained when deprivation of employment opportunities (X_1), educational facilities (X_2), health facilities (X_3), social ties (X_5), and climate (X_6) are controlled. Thus, the original relationship of .31 between deprivation of housing facilities and predisposition to move is spurious and caused by deprivation of employment opportunities, health facilities, education facilities, social ties, and climate. Consequently, the hypothesis is not upheld, that is, deprivation of housing facilities at the area of residence does not contribute appreciably to predisposition to move.

Effects of Deprivation of Social Ties on
Predisposition to Move for Better Social Ties

Hypothesis 5

Assuming better social relations at the area of destination, predisposition to move is positively related to deprivation of social relations at the area of residence.

Data in Table 10 do not support the hypothesized relationship. On the contrary, the partial correlation coefficient of -.18 indicates a slight but significant negative relationship between deprivation of social ties and predisposition to move for better social ties, which is in the opposite direction predicted in the hypothesis.

TABLE 10

RELATIONSHIP BETWEEN DEPRIVATION OF SOCIAL TIES (X_5) AND PREDISPOSITION TO MOVE FOR BETTER SOCIAL TIES (X_{11})

Measure of Relationship	Strength of Relationship	Level of Significance
Pearson $r_{11,5}$	.17*	.05
Kendall tau 11,5	.25**	
$R_{11.1,2,3,4,5,6}$	.48*	.05
$R^2_{11.1,2,3,4,5,6}$	.23*	
$r_{11,5.1,2,3,4,6}$	-.18*	.05
$r^2_{11,5.1,2,3,4,6}$	.03*	

       * Sample size: 118.

       **Sample size: 333.

In view of the unexpected negative relationship between deprivation of social ties and predisposition to move, one may question the validity of the present findings since most previous research studies emphasize the importance of family and community ties in a rural setting and the strong attachment of rural people to their community and kin. However, a careful examination of the question asked respondents, namely, the way the deprivation was measured, would lead one not to be startled by these results. For example, deprivation of social ties was measured in terms of dissatisfaction with friends and relatives, and predisposition to move was measured in terms of willingness to move to another area where there are friends and relatives. The slight negative relationship between the two variables should now be clear and anticipated. That is, persons who have unsatisfactory relationships with their present relatives and friends, as contrasted with those who have satisfactory relationships, would be less likely to move to another area where there are other relatives and friends.

In view of the present findings, one should take another look at the notion of the importance of family and community ties on rural people's predisposition to move and migration. Migration in the direction where there are relatives and friends does not necessarily mean that people go for that purpose.

Effects of Deprivation of Climate on Predisposition to Move for Better Climate

Hypothesis 6

> Assuming better climate at the area of destination, predisposition to move is positively related to deprivation of climate at the area of residence.

This hypothesis is highly supported. Simple, multiple, and partial correlations indicate strong relationships between deprivation of climate (X_6) and predisposition to move for better climate (X_{12}) (Table 11).

A multiple correlation of .58 was obtained when the effects of all six independent variables were included. The partial relationship between deprivation of climate and predisposition to move dropped slightly and insignificantly to .49 after removing the effects of the other five variables.

In view of these findings, the hypothesis is highly supported. That is, deprivation of climate is positively and causally related to predisposition to move, with the former contributing an average of 18 per cent of the total variance of predisposition to move.

Relationships Between Predisposition to Move
and Plans to Migrate

<u>Hypothesis 7</u>

Predisposition to move is positively related to plans to migrate.

The aim in examining this hypothesis is to determine the type of causal relationship between predisposition to move and plans to migrate. That is, is predisposition to move a necessary or sufficient condition or both for plans to migrate?

TABLE 11

RELATIONSHIP BETWEEN DEPRIVATION OF CLIMATE (X_6) ON
PREDISPOSITION TO MOVE FOR BETTER CLIMATE (X_{12})

Measure of Relationship	Strength of Relationship	Level of Significance
Pearson $r_{12,6}$	.44*	.05
Kendall tau 12,6	.48**	.05
$R_{12.1,2,3,4,5,6}$	.58*	.05
$R^2_{12.1,2,3,4,5,6}$	.34*	
$r_{12,6.1,2,3,4,5}$	.49*	.05
$r^2_{12,6.1,2,3,4,5}$	.24*	

* Sample size: 118.

**Sample size: 333.

As indicated earlier in the analysis of time order between the three stages of migration, there are significant statistical relationships between plans to migrate and predisposition to move for better employment opportunities (.21), educational facilities (.18), health facilities (.30), housing facilities (.33), social ties (.33), and climate (.27) considered one at a time. The respondents were also asked a general question about their predisposition to move for all these reasons considered together.

A two-way frequency distribution of general predisposition to move and plans to migrate reveals that all of those who had plans to migrate were predisposed to move, and, conversely, none of those who were not predisposed to move had any plans to migrate, giving support to the hypothesis: plans to migrate and predisposition to move are positively related and, furthermore, predisposition to move is a necessary but not sufficient condition for plans to migrate (Table 12).

TABLE 12

DISTRIBUTION OF RESPONDENTS BY PLANS TO MIGRATE AND
PREDISPOSITION TO MOVE FOR BETTER: EMPLOYMENT OPPORTUNITIES,
HEALTH FACILITIES, EDUCATIONAL FACILITIES, HOUSING,
SOCIAL TIES, AND CLIMATE

		Plans to Move		
		No	Do Not Know	Yes
Predisposition to Move	No	80	3	0
	Do Not Know	36	3	0
	Yes	148	29	21

In view of the above findings, it may be concluded that plans to migrate are contingent on specific other factors, such as income, education, etc., which are considered below.

Effects of Economic Status, Family Size, Liquidity of Assets, Education, Occupational Skills, Age, Employment Status, and Sex on Plans to Migrate

The object of this section is to determine under what conditions persons predisposed to move will or can migrate, for as has been demonstrated in the preceding section not all persons desiring to move have plans to migrate.

It is hypothesized that plans to migrate are affected by both predisposition to move and other socioeconomic factors, depending on the type of migration: migration for general purposes and migration for employment purposes.[3]

In general migration, it is assumed that plans to migrate are related to the cost of move and financial ability of the respondent to make the move. These include family size, possession of fixed assets, and economic status. In the case of migration for employment purposes, plans to migrate are affected by the cost of the move and financial ability as well as the following factors: education, age, professional skills, employment status, and sex.

Effects of Economic Status on Plans to Migrate

Hypothesis 8

Among those predisposed to move, plans to migrate are positively related to economic status.

Table 13 shows a nonsignificant relationship (.03) between plans to migrate (X_{21}) and economic status (X_{13}). The hypothesis is not supported: there is no relationship between plans to migrate and economic status.

Effects of Family Size on Plans to Migrate

Hypothesis 9

Among those predisposed to move, plans to migrate are negatively related to family size.

The zero order association between plans to migrate (X_{21}) and family size (X_{14}) is .03, which is insignificant at the 5 per cent level (Table 13). The hypothesis is not supported: plans to migrate are not related to family size.

TABLE 13

ZERO ORDER GAMMAS FOR PLANS TO MIGRATE (X_{21}) AND
OTHER VARIABLES IN THE MODEL OF THOSE
PREDISPOSED TO MOVE*

Other Variables		Plans to Migrate (X_{21})	Level of Significance
X_{13}	Economic Status	.03	.05
X_{14}	Family Size	.03	.05
X_{15}	Liquidity of Assets	.05	.05

* Sample size: 209.

Effects of Liquidity of Assets on Plans to Migrate

Hypothesis 10

Among those predisposed to move, plans to migrate are negatively related to possession of fixed assets.

Test results in Table 13 fail to support the hypothesis. The relationship between plans to migrate (X_{21}) and liquidity of assets (X_{15}) is
.05, which is insignificant at the 5 per cent level. Consequently, plans
to migrate and liquidity of assets are not related.

Effects of Education, Occupational Skills, Age, Employment Status, and Sex on Plans to Migrate of Those Desiring to Move for Employment Purposes

Effects of Education on Plans to Migrate

Hypothesis 11

For those predisposed to move for better employment opportunities, plans to migrate are positively related to education.

It can be observed from Table 14 that the data do not support the predicted relationship, but rather show a slight negative association between
plans to migrate (X_{21}) and education (X_{16}) (G = -.17).

This relationship is significant at the .05 level for one-tail hypothesis but is not significant for two-tail hypothesis. Since the degree of
association between education and plans to migrate is very weak, it is not
of theoretical significance. Thus, it may be concluded that plans to
migrate are not related to education.

Effects of Occupational Skills on Plans to Migrate

Hypothesis 12

For those predisposed to move for better employment opportunities, plans to migrate are positively related to occupational
skills.

The zero order coefficient of association (G = .22) between plans to
migrate (X_{21}) and occupational skills (X_{17}) shown in Table 14 is weak but
statistically significant (P = .05).

TABLE 14

ZERO ORDER GAMMAS FOR PLANS TO MIGRATE (X_{21}) AND OTHER VARIABLES IN THE MODEL OF THOSE PREDISPOSED TO MOVE FOR BETTER EMPLOYMENT OPPORTUNITIES*

Other Variables		Plans to Migrate (X_{21})	Level of Significance
X_{16}	Education	-.17	.05
X_{17}	Occupational Skills	.22	.05
X_{18}	Age	-.02	.05
X_{19}	Employment Status	-.08	.05
X_{20}	Sex	-.01	.05

* Sample size: 94.

An examination of Table 14 reveals that no other factor is strongly or significantly related to plans to migrate; consequently, no control will be used and the hypothesis is considered upheld. That is, plans to migrate for better employment opportunities are positively related to occupational skills.

Effects of Age on Plans to Migrate

Hypothesis 13

For those predisposed to move for better employment opportunities, plans to migrate are negatively related to labor age.

The data in Table 14 do not lend support for the predicted relationship in the hypothesis. Examination of the zero order correlation ($G = -.02$) indicates the absence of association between plans to migrate and age.

Effects of Employment Status on Plans to Migrate

Hypothesis 14

For those predisposed to move for better employment opportunities, plans to migrate are more common among the unemployed.

The data fail to support the hypothesized relationship. The degree of association between employment status and plans to migrate (G = -.08) is not significant at the 5 per cent level (Table 14). Therefore, it may be concluded that plans to migrate and unemployment are not related.

Effects of Sex on Plans to Migrate

Hypothesis 15

For those predisposed to move for better employment opportunities, plans to migrate are more common among males than females.

Test results in Table 14 fail to support the hypothesis. The coefficient of association between plans to migrate and sex (G = .01) is not significant at the 5 percent level, indicating that there is no relationship between plans to migrate and sex.

In summary, data analysis reveals that plans to migrate are only positively related to occupational skills. On the other hand, economic status, family size, liquidity of assets, education, age, employment status, and sex are not significantly related to plans to migrate.

Footnotes

1. Roy G. Francis, "Some Elementary Logic." An Introduction to Social Research, 2nd ed., ed., John T. Doby (New York: Appleton-Century-Crofts, 1967).

2. For an excellent discussion, see Quinn McNemar, Psychological Statistics (New York, 1963); Mordecai Ezekiel and Karl A. Fox, Methods of Correlation and Regression Analysis (New York, 1959).

3. General migration refers to persons desiring to move for any reason or reasons, while migration for employment purposes refers to those desiring to move for better employment opportunities only.

CHAPTER VI

SUMMARY AND CONCLUSIONS

The purpose of this study has been to determine the stages and factors underlying the decision-making process in voluntary migration as well as the importance of these factors on predisposition to move and migration.

The theoretical migration model consists of three stages: deprivation, predisposition to move, and migration. Each stage is viewed as a necessary but not sufficient condition for the stage following it. Deprivation is assumed to have been caused by factors outside the system - exogenous variables. The major hypotheses concerning the other two stages - predisposition to move and migration - are:

1. Predisposition to move is in part a function of felt deprivation in area of residence of one's wants and perception of opportunities in area of destination to satisfy these wants: employment opportunities, educational facilities, health facilities, social and community ties, housing facilities, and climate.

2. Migration, here measured in terms of plans to migrate, is affected by both predisposition to move and other socioeconomic factors, depending on the type of migration: migration for general purposes and migration for employment opportunities.

   a. In general migration, plans to migrate are related to cost of move and financial ability of the respondent to make the move. These include family size, possession of fixed assets, and economic status.

   b. In migration for employment opportunities, plans to migrate are affected by cost of the move and financial ability as well as by the following factors: education, age, professional skills, employment status, and sex.

The major findings are summarized below.

1. There is a positive and significant relationship, with other related factors being controlled, between predisposition to move and each of deprivation of employment opportunities, educational facilities, health facilities, and climate, which suggests that deprivation of these

factors induces people to be predisposed to move. The relative importance of each of these factors on predisposition to move, in terms of the strength of relationship and percentage of variance explained, is as follows in order of decreasing importance: deprivation of climate, deprivation of educational facilities, deprivation of health facilities, and deprivation of employment opportunities.

There is a slight negative relationship between deprivation of social ties and predisposition to move, and there is no relationship between deprivation of housing facilities and predisposition to move.

2. General predisposition to move is positively related to plans to migrate. However, many of those predisposed to move did not have plans to migrate, which suggests that predisposition to move is at best a necessary but not sufficient condition for plans to migrate, and that plans to migrate are contingent on other factors as well.

3. Occupational skills are positively related to plans to migrate for those who are predisposed to move for employment opportunities. No relationship was found, however, between plans to migrate and family size, liquidity of assets, economic status, education, employment status, age, and sex.

4. Data from tabular analysis while consistent with the sequential three-stage model, are also consistent with an alternative explanation: deprivation, predisposition to move, and plans to migrate form a continuum of dissatisfaction with local conditions.

Verification of the sequential model by the recursive system analysis for each of six specific factors - employment opportunities, educational facilities, health facilities, housing facilities, social ties, and climate - is supported only for employment opportunities, housing facilities, and social ties. The analysis is inconclusive in regard to climate, and the three stages model is not supported in respect to educational facilities and health facilities.

For educational facilities, the data support two alternative hypotheses equally well, namely, either: (a) deprivation independently causes predisposition to move and plans to migrate, but predisposition to move does not lead to plans to migrate, or (b) predisposition to move stimulates deprivation, which leads to plans to move. The crucial factor in the choice of these alternative hypotheses is the time order of deprivation and predisposition to move. As this information is not available, an inference as to the most probable model cannot be made.

In like manner, for climate and health facilities the data lend support to either of two alternative hypotheses: (a) predisposition to move causes both deprivation and plans to migrate, or (b) deprivation causes both predisposition to move and plans to migrate.

In view of the inconclusive evidence of establishing time order between deprivation, predisposition to move, and plans to migrate, the possibility of another alternative hypothesis is raised: deprivation, predisposition to move, and plans to migrate represent a continuum of dissatisfaction with local conditions whereby "predisposition to move" signifies a stronger dissatisfaction than "deprivation," and "plans to migrate" signify still a stronger dissatisfaction. Although this alternative hypothesis is more supported by the data in the sense that it does not require time order, the original three-stage model is more powerful theoretically. But again, present information is not sufficient to determine which is the most plausible hypothesis. Only further research can resolve this issue.

Limitations of Findings and Implications
for Further Research

The validity and generalizability of the above results and the adequacy and applicability of the theoretical model are contingent on the nature of the study population, measurement of variables, and statistical tests used. Accordingly, judgment of the present findings should be made with caution regarding three major problems: (a) level of attitude versus developmental sequence of deprivation, predisposition to move, and plans to migrate; (b) inconsistency of general and specific level results; and (c) failure to find factors correlating with plans to migrate. Looking at the study in retrospect, the following factors have made a conclusive evaluation of the model difficult.

First, as noted in the Methodology chapter, the study area has experienced a heavy population loss from out-migration during the last two decades. As a consequence, many of the persons who desired to move and were able to do so had already migrated, leaving behind mainly those not desiring to move and/or unable to migrate. Thus, the population under study is largely composed of persons lacking many of the basic characteristics that make migration possible, namely, economic status, education, and occupational skills. For example, the majority of the respondents (78 percent) had not gone beyond eighth grade; less than eighteen percent of the families had a gross income over $5,000; and very few of the respondents possessed skills that would enable them to enter the labor market other than in mining. Furthermore, the crucial factor of economic status, which largely determines one's financial ability to make the move, was inadequately measured. The person's savings or ability to borrow money from the bank or friends should be determined as well as his annual income. Only the latter was obtained in this study.

Secondly, the migration model is intended to explain actual migration instead of plans to move as was the case in this study. Ideally, the model should be tested on those who have migrated and those who remain behind, instead of the latter persons alone, as this provides the greatest variation in the personal and socioeconomic characteristics upon which the model is based.

Thirdly, the measures of association used for analyzing the data were Pearson's product moment correlation, Goodman and Kruskal's measure for ordinal association - gamma, and Kendall rank correlation coefficient. These tests measure the "monotomic" relationships implied in the theoretical model, that is, an increase in "x" variable produces an increase in "y" variable. In addition to independence of observations and ordinal measurement that are required by all three tests, the Pearson product moment correlation requires a normal distribution. Because not all variables in this study were normally distributed and some were measured more crudely than others, the size of association is in part a product of the imprecision of measurement and distribution of population. Consequently, judging the relative importance of these variables in terms of their degree of association may be misleading and should be done with some reservations.

Application of the recursive system for analysis of causal model of the form A———➤B———➤C, should be approached with caution in the absence of a perfect correlation between each pair of adjacent variables. In such a case, other variables than A and B are at work in affecting B and C, which could distort the predicted relationships assumed in the model. Furthermore, statistical control of B does not eliminate its interaction effects with A on C. Consequently, the relationship between A and C is not likely to disappear, as predicted by the recursive system, when B is statistically controlled. A frequency distribution, as used in this study, yields a better picture of what is happening.

In a nonexperimental design and a cross-sectional study such as the present one, it is extremely difficult to establish time order and consequently direction of causality between deprivation, predisposition to move and plans to migrate. A longitudinal study is more likely to resolve this issue.

A note of caution should also be made regarding the limitations and interpretation of tests of association. McNemar mentions five methods or ways for interpreting the correlation coefficient.[1] In social science we are generally interested in the strength of association, that is, the degree to which a variation in one variable is associated with variation in another variable. A less than one-to-one relationship, however, may be due to a variety of combinations of distribution of the characteristics of the variables involved. For example, the low degree of correlation between predisposition to move and plans to migrate could have been the result of any of the following conditions: (1) some of those who were predisposed to move did not have any plans to migrate; (2) some of those who were not predisposed to move had plans to migrate; or (3) both conditions 1 and 2. The situation was clarified by a two-way frequency distribution, which showed that the low degree of association resulted from the second condition only, that is, absence of plans to migrate among those predisposed to move, for none of those who were not predisposed to move had any plans to migrate. Thus, the nature of the relationship and the direction of causality between predisposition to move and plans to migrate are clear.

Further analysis is needed regarding the relationships between deprivation in the area of residence, availability of opportunities in the area of destination, and predisposition to move. This study centered on the effects of deprivation of the various factors on predisposition to move for better opportunities, taken one factor at a time. No attempt was made to evaluate the effects of all possible combinations of these factors on predisposition to move. That is, migrants may sacrifice certain less important needs or opportunities in the area of residence to obtain other more salient ones in the area of destination. For example, a person may be willing to leave an area of low employment opportunities, but of good educational and health facilities, to another area of better employment opportunities but of poorer educational and health facilities. Such an analysis will be highly valuable to better understanding the relative importance of the various factors involved in the decision-making process to move.

Finally, like all studies in the social sciences, this study is in need of replication to determine the validity of its basic assumptions and to increase confidence in its results.

Implications for Policy

One of the major objectives of the Campbell County Project, for which the initial data were collected, was to determine under what conditions the isolated rural people studied can be induced to move to adjacent areas where better services in terms of job opportunities, educational facilities, health facilities, housing, water supply, and sewage facilities are or could be made available.

The findings of the present study strongly suggest that both dissatisfaction with conditions at the area of residence and availability of opportunities at the area of destination, namely, employment opportunities, educational facilities, health facilities, and climate, play an important part in people's predisposition to move and plans to migrate. Furthermore, neither dissatisfaction with conditions at the area of residence nor availability of opportunities at the area of destination alone is sufficient to induce a significant predisposition to move or plans to migrate. Thus, both conditions at the area of residence and destination must be taken into account by change agencies attempting to encourage people to move from or stay in their communities or neighborhoods. It follows that if the purpose of a public organization is to encourage people to remain in their communities, then efforts should be made to improve the local conditions to the utmost satisfaction of the residents. If, on the other hand, the purpose is to induce people to move, efforts should be made to improve conditions at the area of destination only. Any other public program or programs that are in operation to help or improve local conditions at the area of residence should be discouraged. Unfortunately, the latter suggestion is most often ignored, for there are always persons and agencies who advocate and help needy people regardless of where they are located or their circumstances.

Clearly, any policy to relocate people, to determine the area of destination, and to provide or deny assistance to the communities involved, require the cooperative efforts of many professionals: economists, planners, and politicians. The role of social scientists should also be clear: they may be able to bring useful evidence to bear upon the attitudes and behavior of the people affected which should be taken into account in any decision-making.

Footnotes

1. Quinn McNemar, Psychological Statistics, 3rd ed. (New York, 1962), pp. 134-35.

CAMPBELL COUNTY DEMONSTRATION PROGRAM
EAST TENNESSEE ECONOMIC DEVELOPMENT DISTRICT

Campbell and Clairborne Counties Migration Study
December, 1968

INTRODUCTORY STATEMENT: My name is_____ We are working for
the East Tennessee Economic Development District in Campbell and Clairborne Counties. We are talking with families in these counties and
getting information about the people's needs and interests and living
conditions. The purpose is to obtain information that will be helpful
in improving living conditions of families in this area of the state.
All information is strictly confidential. Your name will not be used
and your answers will not be given to anyone else. I would like to
talk with you for a few minutes about some of these things if you don't
mind.

Interviewer_____ Call Back 1._____
                                                                  Date

Date_____
                                                              2._____
                                                                  Date
Name of Head of Household_____

                                                              3._____
Phone Number of Head of Household_____   Date

IBM	Code	Question
1	1	Card Number_____
2,3,4		Schedule Number_____

(INTERVIEWER: Circle, check, or fill out answers
to the following questions and then code them where
it applies.)

IBM	Code	Question

5   1. Postal Routes:
- 1 La Follette
- 2 Duff
- 3 Morley
- 4 Caryville
- 5 Pioneer
- 6 Elk Valley
- 7 Clairfield and Eagan

6   2. Sex:
- 1 Male
- 2 Female

7   3. Marital Status:
- 1 Single
- 2 Married
- 3 Widowed
- 4 Divorced
- 5 Separated

8   4. How old are you?_____Years
- 1 19 or Under
- 2 20 - 24 Years
- 3 25 - 29 Years
- 4 30 - 34 Years
- 5 35 - 44 Years
- 6 45 - 54 Years
- 7 55 - 64 Years
- 8 65 - 74 Years
- 9 75 or Over

9   5. What was the highest grade or year you completed in school?
- 1 No Education
- 2   1   2   3 Grade
- 3   4   5   6 Grade
- 4   7   8   Grade
- 5   9   10   Grade
- 6   11   12   Grade
- 7   1   2   Years of College
- 8   3   4   Years of College
- 9 Postgraduate

IBM	Code	Question

10   **6.** What is your present employment status?
1   Full-time employed
2   Part-time employed
3   Unemployed
4   Retired
5   Student
6   Military
7   Housewife

11,12   a.   (<u>INTERVIEWER</u>:   If respondent is employed full or part-time, ask:)   What kind(s) of work you do?

_____

_____

13   b.   (<u>INTERVIEWER</u>:   If respondent is unemployed, ask:) Why are you not employed? _____

_____

7. Next, I would like to ask you some questions about the places in which you have lived and the kind of work you have done. Starting with your present job and working back as far as you can remember, will you please name these jobs and places in which you spent 2 or more months?

	Kind(s) of Work	City	State
1.			
2.			
3.			
4.			
5.			
6.			
7.			
8.			
9.			
10.			

(<u>INTERVIEWER</u>:   From information in above table, code the following:)

14   a.   Number of different places (communities) in which respondent lived (Code actual number; Code 9 if 9 or more places are mentioned)

93

IBM	Code	Question
15		b. Number of different jobs held (Code actual number; code 9 if 9 or more different jobs are mentioned)

LIVING ARRANGEMENT

16		8. Where were you born?

0   Not Applicable (Don't know, no answer)
1   In this neighborhood
2   In another neighborhood

17		9. How long have you been living in this neighborhood?

1   4 Years
2   5 - 9 Years
3   10 - 14 Years
4   15 - 19 Years
5   20 - 24 Years
6   25 - 29 Years
7   30 or more Years

18		10. How long have you been living in this house?

1   4 Years
2   5 - 9 Years
3   10 - 14 Years
4   15 - 19 Years
5   20 - 24 Years
6   25 - 29 Years

19		11. Do you own this house, rent it, or live free in it?

1   Own House
2   Rent House
3   Live free in House

20		12. How many rooms do you have in your house (Do not count bathrooms, halls, or unimproved basements)?

_____Rooms

(INTERVIEWER: Code actual number of rooms; code 9 for 9 or more rooms)

IBM	Code	Question

21   **13.** How many people are living in this house?_____
No. of people

(INTERVIEWER: Include respondent plus all of others living in household with family at time of interview and taking part in household activities - eating and sleeping - during last three months. Code actual number of people; code 9 for 9 or more people)

22   a. How many of these are your own children?
_____Children

(INTERVIEWER: Code actual number of children; code 9 for 9 or more children)

    1. What are their ages?

1.____Years		6.____Years	
2.____Years		7.____Years	
3.____Years		8.____Years	
4.____Years		9.____Years	
5.____Years		10.____Years	

(INTERVIEWER: From the above information in Q. 13a.1., code the following:)

23   a. Number of teenagers (18 or under)

24   b. Number of adult children (19 or over)

(INTERVIEWER: Code actual number; code 9 for 9 or more children)

25   b. How many of these are relatives other than children?
_____Children

(INTERVIEWER: Include all sons and daughters-in-laws, in-laws, relatives, and any other permanent member. Code actual number; code 9 for 9 or more persons)

    1. What are their ages and kind of work they do?

	Age	Type of work
1.	____Years	_____
2.	____Years	_____
3.	____Years	_____
4.	____Years	_____
5.	____Years	_____
6.	____Years	_____

(INTERVIEWER: From the above information in Q.
13b.1., code the following)

26   a. Number of teenagers (18 or under)

27   b. Number of adults (19 or over)

28   c. Number of working adults

29,30   14. Now would you please tell me which of the following
                 pieces of equipment and household items you have?
                 ____Car: Year of make 19_____
                 ____Car: Year of Make 19_____
                 ____Car: Year of Make 19_____
                 ____Central Heating
                 ____Piped Water in House
                 ____Washing Machine
                 ____Indoor Flush Toilet
                 ____Indoor Bath or Shower
                 ____Electric Vacuum Cleaner
                 ____Piano
                 ____Dishwasher
                 ____Electric Range
                 ____Air Conditioner
                 ____Telephone
                 ____F.M. or Shortwave Radio
                 ____Record Player
                 ____Power Lawn Mower
                 ____Boat
                 ____Home Freezer
                 ____Television

                 (INTERVIEWER: Code total score by giving a
                 score of 1 to any possession of an item)

ATTITUDES TOWARD MIGRATION

(INTERVIEWER: Read to the respondent the following: The
next few questions are somewhat hard to understand, and
it is very important that you understand them well before
answering them. So, please don't hesitate to ask us to

IBM	Code	Question

repeat any question as many times as needed till you are sure you understand it well.)

31

15. What kind of place do you prefer to live in? Would you prefer to live in: (INTERVIEWER: Read to respondent first 4 choices only)
   1   Open Country Farm
   2   Mountain, Open Country Non-Farm
   3   Town or Small City
   4   Big City, or
   5   It Doesn't Matter, Anywhere (Undecided)

32

16. If you could choose, where would you prefer to live when you get too old to work? (INTERVIEWER: if respondent is old and not employed, ask: Now that you are too old to work, where would you prefer to live?)
   1   Here
   2   Anywhere, It Doesn't Matter, Hard to Say
   3   Someplace Else (INTERVIEWER: If Someplace Else, ask where. If respondent doesn't give any place at all then put him under "anywhere" category.)
   a. _____
      City or Town   County
      _____
               State or Region

33

(INTERVIEWER: Indicate into which of the following categories the place mentioned falls:)
   0   Not Applicable (If answer is here or anywhere, it doesn't matter)
   1   Some Place of Residence
   2   Another Community Within This County
   3   Elsewhere in the State
   4   Elsewhere in the U.S.
   5   Foreign Country
   6   Anywhere, It Doesn't Matter

34

17. If you could choose, where would you prefer to be buried?
   1   Here, This Neighborhood
   2   Anywhere, It Doesn't Matter, Hard to Say
   3   Someplace Else (INTERVIEWER: If Someplace Else, ask where. If respondent doesn't give any place at all then put him under "Anywhere" category)
   a. _____
      City or Town   County
      _____
               State or Region

IBM	Code	Question

35   (<u>INTERVIEWER</u>: Indicate into which of the following categories the place mentioned falls:)

         0   Not Applicable (If answer is here or any-where, it doesn't matter)
         1   Some Place of Residence
         2   Another Community Within this County
         3   Elsewhere in the State
         4   Elsewhere in the Country
         5   Foreign Country
         6   Anywhere, It Doesn't Matter

36   18.   Do you ever wish you were living in another area?
         1   No
         2   Undecided, No Answer
         3   Yes

37   19.   If you could, would you like to move to some other place to live?
         1   No
         2   Don't Know, Not Sure, It Depends
         3   Yes

38   a.   (<u>INTERVIEWER</u>: If answer is <u>No</u>, ask:) Why not?_____

_____

39   1.   (Then ask:) How about if you are pro-vided with a good job and nice house that is close to schools, doctors, and hospitals would you then be willing to move?
         0   No Applicable (If answer to Q.19 is <u>Yes</u>, <u>Don't Know</u>, It Depends, or Not Sure.)
         1   No
         2   Maybe
         3   Yes

        b.   (<u>INTERVIEWER</u>: If answer to Q.19 is <u>Don't Know</u>, <u>Not Sure</u>, or <u>It Depends</u>, ask:) Why do you say that or it depends on what?____

_____

41   c.   (<u>INTERVIEWER</u>: If answer to Q.19 is <u>Yes</u>, ask:)
         1.   Why would you like to leave?_____

_____

IBM	Code	Question

42

    2. (Then ask:) Why haven't you moved to another place so far?_____

    3. (Then ask:) Where would you like to go? _____
                                  City

        County   State

43

(INTERVIEWER: Indicate into which of the following categories the place mentioned falls)
0   Not Applicable (If answer to Q.19 is No, Don't Know, It Depends)
1   Same Place of Residence
2   Another Community Within this County
3   Elsewhere in the State
4   Elsewhere in the U.S.
5   Foreign Country
6   Anywhere, It Doesn't Matter

44

20. If you were given the opportunity by being offered a good paying job and a nice house, which of the following towns of Campbell County would you like to live in?
1   La Follete
2   Jellico
3   Caryville
4   Jacksboro
5   None, Will Not Move

45

21. Would you be interested in living in a newly constructed city somewhere in Campbell County if you were offered a good job and a nice house?
1   No
2   Don't Know, It Depends
3   Yes

46

22. Do you plan on moving to another area sometime in the near future?
1   No
2   Not Sure, It Depends, Maybe
3   Yes

47

23. Migration Index (Add Columns 36, 37, 45, and 46) and 74 of Card #1

IBM	Code	Question

Question

24. Next, I am going to give you a list of six things that people who move to other places think about when they move. Will you please tell me which one you think is most important, which one is second most important and so on? (INTERVIEWER: Pass on card to respondent, then code each category as ranked by respondent.)
Rank

48 _____Good Doctors and Hospitals

49 _____Good Teachers and Schools

50 _____Nice Home and Furnishings, and Good Clean Neighborhood

51 _____Acquaintances, Relatives, Friends, and Social Activities

52 _____A Pleasant and Good Paying Job

53 _____Nice Climate and Weather

54 25. As far as you are concerned, what do you consider as the most important to have where you live? (INTERVIEWER: Read slowly to respondent first two choices only or pass on card to respondent.)
  1 Good Schools, Teachers, Doctors, and Hospitals or
  2 The Kind of Job and the Wage Paid
  3 Hard to Say, Both are Equally Important

55 26. If it were up to you alone and no one else, in which one of the following places would you prefer to live? (INTERVIEWER: Pass on card to respondent and read to him slowly. Repeat question if necessary until respondent seems to understand it.)
  1 Where your earnings will remain the same as you are making here, but the schools, teachers, doctors, and hospitals are better than here, or
  2 Where your earnings will be higher than you are making here, but the schools, teachers, doctors, and hospitals are the same as around here, or
  3 Would rather stay and live right here.

IBM	Code	Question		1 No	2 Don't Know, It Depends, Maybe, Hard To Say	3 Yes
56	27.	a.	If you could, would you move to another area which has better Doctors and Hospitals than are around here?	_____	_____	_____
57		b.	If you could, would you move to another area which has better Doctors and Hospitals than are around here, but with everything else being worse off than here?	_____	_____	_____
58		c.	If you could, would you move to another area which has better Doctors and Hospitals than are around here, but with everything else remaining the same as here?	_____	_____	_____
59	28.	a.	If you could, would you move to another area which has better teachers and schools than are around here?	_____	_____	_____
60		b.	If you could, would you move to another area which has better teachers and schools than are around here, but with everything else being worse off than here?	_____	_____	_____

IBM	Code	Question	1 No	2 Don't Know, It Depends, Maybe, Hard to Say	3 Yes
61		c.	If you could, would you move to another area which has better teachers and schools than are around here, <u>but with everything else remaining the same as here?</u> ____	____	____
62	29.	a.	If you could, would you move to another area where you will have a nicer home and furnishings, and a good clean neighborhood than are around here? ____	____	____
63		b.	If you could, would you move to another area where you will have a better home and furnishings, and a good clean neighborhood than are around here, <u>but with everything else being worse off than here?</u> ____	____	____
64		c.	If you could, would you move to another area where you will have a nicer home and furnishings, and a cleaner neighborhood than you have around here, <u>but with everything else remaining the same as here?</u> ____	____	____
65	30.	a.	If you could, would you move to another area where you would have a better paying and more pleasant job than around here? ____	____	____

IBM	Code	Question			1 No	2 Don't Know, It Depends, Maybe, Hard to Say	3 Yes
66	30.	b.	If you could, would you move to another area where you would have a better paying and more pleasant job than around here, but with everything else being worse off than here?		___	___	___
67		c.	If you could, would you move to another area where you would have a better paying and more pleasant job than around here, but with everything else remaining the same as here?		___	___	___
68	31.	a.	If you could, would you move to another area which has a better climate and weather than here?		___	___	___
69		b.	If you could would you move to another area which has a better climate and weather than here, but with everything else being worse off than here?		___	___	___
70		c.	If you could, would you move to another area which has a better climate and weather than here, but with everything else remaining the same as here?		___	___	___

IBM	Code	Question	1 No	2 Don't Know, It Depends, Maybe, Hard to Say	3 Yes
71		32. a. If you could, would you move to another area where you would have a good deal more acquaintances, relatives, friends, and social activities than you have around here?	_____	_____	_____
72		b. If you could, would you move to another area where you would have a good deal more acquaintances, relatives, friends, and social activities than you have around here, <u>but with everything else being worse off than here?</u>	_____	_____	_____
73		c. If you could, would you move to another area where you would have a good deal more acquaintances, relatives, friends, and social activities than you have around here, <u>but with everything else being the same as here?</u>	_____	_____	_____
74		33. a. If you could, would you move to another area where you would have a better job, better Doctors and Hospitals, better Teachers and Schools and nicer home and furnishings, and a cleaner neighborhood than are around here?	_____	_____	_____

SATISFACTION WITH PRESENT NEIGHBORHOOD AND
LIVING CONDITIONS

75   **34.** How far is the place where you work from your home?
                        _____ Minutes

                 0   Not Applicable (Don't Work)
                 1   1 - 5 Minutes
                 2   6 - 10 Minutes
                 3   11 - 20 Minutes
                 4   21 - 30 Minutes
                 5   31 - 40 Minutes
                 6   41 - 50 Minutes
                 7   51 - 60 Minutes
                 8   Over one hour

76   **35.** How far is the school from your home?
                       _____ Minutes

                 0   Not Applicable (Don't have children going to school)
                 1   1 - 5 Minutes
                 2   6 - 10 Minutes
                 3   11 - 20 Minutes
                 4   21 - 30 Minutes
                 5   31 - 40 Minutes
                 6   41 - 50 Minutes
                 7   51 - 60 Minutes
                 8   Over one hour

77   **36.** How far is your Doctor from home? _____ Minutes
                 1   1 - 5 Minutes
                 2   6 - 10 Minutes
                 3   11 - 20 Minutes
                 4   21 - 30 Minutes
                 5   31 - 40 Minutes
                 6   41 - 50 Minutes
                 7   51 - 60 Minutes
                 8   Over one hour

IBM	Code	Question

78   37.   How far is the Hospital from your home:
_____ Minutes
1   1 - 5 Minutes
2   6 - 10 Minutes
3   11 - 20 Minutes
4   21 - 30 Minutes
5   31 - 40 Minutes
6   41 - 50 Minutes
7   51 - 60 Minutes
8   Over one hour

79   38.   How far is the church from your home?
_____ Minutes
0   Not Applicable (Don't go to church)
1   1 - 5 Minutes
2   6 - 10 Minutes
3   11 - 20 Minutes
4   21 - 30 Minutes
5   31 - 40 Minutes
6   41 - 50 Minutes
7   51 - 60 Minutes
8   Over one hour

80   39.   How far is your closest friend from your home?
_____ Minutes
1   1 - 5 Minutes
2   6 - 10 Minutes
3   11 - 20 Minutes
4   21 - 30 Minutes
5   31 - 40 Minutes
6   41 - 50 Minutes
7   51 - 60 Minutes
8   Over one hour

1   2   Card Number

2,3,4   Schedule Number

(INTERVIEWER: Circle, check or fill out answers to the
following questions and then code them where it applies.)

106

IBM	Code	Question

40. Next, I am going to ask you a few questions regarding your satisfaction with life around here. (<u>INTERVIEWER</u>: pass on card to respondent for the next 14 questions.)

	1	2	3	4	5
	Very Sat- isfied	Pretty Sat- isfied	About Aver- age	Some- what Unsat- isfied	Very Unsat- isfied

5   **a.** On the whole how satisfied are you with your way of life around here? ___ ___ ___ ___ ___

6   **b.** How sat- isfied are you with your pres- ent job(s)? ___ ___ ___ ___ ___
          0   Not Applicable (Don't Work)

7   **c.** How sat- isfied are you with the income or salary you earn from this job? ___ ___ ___ ___ ___
          0   Not Applicable (Don't Work)

8   **d.** How satis- fied are you with the ser- vices you get from doctors around here? ___ ___ ___ ___ ___

IBM	Code	Question	1 Very Sat- isfied	2 Pretty Sat- isfied	3 About Aver- age	4 Some- what Unsat- isfied	5 Very Unsat- isfied
9	e.	How satis- fied are you with the hospi- tals(s) around here?	_____	_____	_____	_____	_____
10	f.	How satis- fied are you with the schools around here?	_____	_____	_____	_____	_____
11	g.	How satis- fied are you with the Tea- chers in these schools?	_____	_____	_____	_____	_____
12	h.	How satis- fied are you with your house?	_____	_____	_____	_____	_____
13	i.	How satis- fied are you with your home furnish- ings?	_____	_____	_____	_____	_____
14	j.	How satis- fied are you with the water supply in your house?	_____	_____	_____	_____	_____

IBM	Code	Question	1	2	3	4	5
			Very Sat- isfied	Pretty Sat- isfied	About Aver- age	Some- what Unsat- isfied	Very Unsat- isfied
15	k.	How satis- fied are you with your re- lations with peo- ple of this neighbor- hood in general?	_____	_____	_____	_____	_____
16	l.	How satis- fied are you with your rela- tions with kinfolks around here?	_____	_____	_____	_____	_____
17	m.	How satis- fied are you with your rela- tions with friends around here?	_____	_____	_____	_____	_____
18.	n.	How satis- fied are you with the wea- ther and climate around here?	_____	_____	_____	_____	_____

(INTERVIEWER: Pass on card to respondent for the next 13 questions.)

IBM	Code	Question	1 Very Good	2 Pretty Good	3 About Aver- age	4 Not Very Good	5 Not Good At All
19	o.	In general, how do you feel about living in this neighborhood? Would you say it is	____	____	____	____	____
20	p.	On the whole, how good do you feel that your job(s) is?	____	____	____	____	____
		0 Not Applicable (Don't Work)					
21	q.	How good do you feel that the income or salary you earn from this job(s) is?	____	____	____	____	____
		0 Not Applicable (Don't Work)					
22	r.	How good is this neighborhood as far as doctors are concerned?	____	____	____	____	____
23	s.	How good is this neighborhood as far as hospitals are concerned?	____	____	____	____	____

IBM	Code	Question	1 Very Good	2 Pretty Good	3 About Aver- age	4 Not Very Good	5 Not Good At All
24		t. How good is this neighborhood as far as schools are concerned?	_____	_____	_____	_____	_____
25		u. How good is this neighborhood as far as teachers in these schools are concerned?	_____	_____	_____	_____	_____
26		v. How good do you feel that your house is?	_____	_____	_____	_____	_____
27		w. How good do you feel that your home furnishings are?	_____	_____	_____	_____	_____
28		x. How well do you get along with your kinfolks around here?	_____	_____	_____	_____	_____

111

IBM	Code	Question	1	2	3	4	5
			Very Good	Pretty Good	About Aver- age	Not Very Good	Not Good At All

29   y.   How well do you get along with your friends and acquain- tances around here? ___   ___   ___   ___   ___

30   z.   How well do you get along with people of this neigh- borhood? ___   ___   ___   ___   ___

31   z.1   How well do you like the climate and weather around here? ___   ___   ___   ___   ___

32,33   General Satisfaction Index (Q. 40.a and o)

34,35   Satisfaction with Job Index (Q. 40.b,c,p and q)

36,37   Satisfaction with Health Facilities Index (Q. 40.d,r and s)

38,39   Satisfaction with Educational Facilities Index (Q. 40.f,g, t and u)

40,41   Satisfaction with House Facilities Index (Q. 40.h,i,j,v and w)

42,43   Satisfaction with Social Relations Index (Q. 40.k,l,m,x,y and z)

44,45   Satisfaction with Weather and Climate Index (Q. 40.n and z.1)

46   41.   What kind of work would you most like to do:_____
       0   Not Applicable (Retired or Invalid)

IBM	Code	Question

47   42. Would you like to learn to do another job?
                        1   Yes
                        2   No

48   a.   (INTERVIEWER: If answer is Yes, ask: What kind(s)?   (List in order of preference.)————————————

                         0   Not Applicable (All those with No answer to Q. 42.)

49   b.   (INTERVIEWER: If answer is No, ask:) How about if you got paid to learn a new job, would you then be interested?
                         0   Not Applicable (All those with "yes" answer to Q. 42.)
                         1   Yes
                         2   No

50   43. When you are not working, what do you enjoy doing most?————————————

51   44. As far as you are concerned, what do you like most about living around here?————————————

52   45. As far as you are concerned, what do you dislike most about living around here?————————————

53   46. If you were asked to name the most important improvement that would make Campbell County a better place in which to live, what would it be?————————————

54   47. If you made an extra $500 this year what would you buy or do with it? ————————————

COMMUNICATION AND SOCIAL PARTICIPATION

55   48. Do you subscribe to or read often any of the following.
                  a.   Newspaper:
                       1   Yes
                       2   No
                       (If yes)   Name of newspaper(s)

IBM	Code	Question

56   b.   Magazine:
                              1   Yes
                              2   No
                              (If yes) Name of magazine(s)

                              _____

57   c.   Pamphlets and Bulletins:
                              1   Yes
                              2   No
                              (If yes)   Name of Pamphlet(s) or Bulle-
                              tin(s)_____

                              _____

58   49.   Do you listen to the radio?
                          1   Yes
                          2   No
                          (If yes)   Which Station(s)_____

                          _____

59   50.   Do you watch TV?
                          1   Yes
                          2   No
                          (If yes)   Which Channel(s)_____

                          _____

       51.   Now, I would like to get a list of the organizations
             you belong to or take part in.

             Do you belong to or take part in:

Name of Organization	Member	How Often Did you Attend Meetings During Past 12 Months		Are You an Officer or Committee Member	Total Score
		Hardly or Never	Regularly or Often		
	3	0	1		1

114

IBM	Code	Question		Member	How Often Did You Attend Meetings During Past 12 Months	Are You an Officer or Committee Member	Total Score
			Name of Organization		Hardly or Never	Regularly or Often	
60		a.	Farm Organization (Farm Bureau, Farmer's Union, Grange, Ag. Soil Conservation, 4-H)				
61		b.	Church				
62		c.	Labor Union				
63		d.	Services or Civic Organizations (Rotary, Kiwanis, PTA, Other)				
64		e.	Lodges or Fraternities (Masons, etc.)				
65		f.	Political Organizations (Precinct Worker, etc.)				
66		g.	Other:				

67   52. About how much of your total income was from your job(s) or rent?

    0   None
    1   1/4 or Less
    2   1/3
    3   1/2
    4   2/3
    5   3/4
    6   All: 100%

IBM	Code	Question

68   53. About how much of your total income was from the sale
         of farm products?
         0   None
         1   1/4 or Less
         2   1/3
         3   1/2
         4   2/3
         5   3/4
         6   All: 100%

69   54. About how much of your total income was from mining?
         0   None
         1   1/4 or Less
         2   1/3
         3   1/2
         4   2/3
         5   3/4
         6   All: 100%

70   55. About how much of your total income was from public
         assistance or welfare?
         0   None
         1   1/4 or Less
         2   1/3
         3   1/2
         4   2/3
         5   3/4
         6   All: 100%

71   56. About how much of your total income was from unemploy-
         ment insurance?
         0   None
         1   1/4 or Less
         2   1/3
         3   1/2
         4   2/3
         5   3/4
         6   All: 100%

72   57. About how much of your total income was from retire-
         ment benefits?
         0   None
         1   1/4 or Less
         2   1/3
         3   1/2
         4   2/3
         5   3/4
         6   All: 100%

73   58.   Other sources of income?

                        0   None
                        1   1/4 or Less
                        2   1/3
                        3   1/2
                        4   2/3
                        5   3/4
                        6   All: 100%

74,75   59.   What was your and your family's total income before
taxes from all sources including jobs, farming, mining,
unemployment insurance, welfare, etc., during the past
year?

(INTERVIEWER: Pass out card to respondent.)

   1   Under $500
   2        $ 500   - $ 999
   3        $ 1,000   - $ 1,999
   4        $ 2,000   - $ 2,999
   5        $ 3,000   - $ 3,999
   6        $ 4,000   - $ 4,999
   7        $ 5,000   - $ 5,999
   8        $ 6,000   - $ 6,999
   9        $ 7,000   - $ 7,999
  10        $ 8,000   - $ 8,999
  11        $ 9,000   - $ 9,999
  12        $10,000   - $10,999
  13        $11,000   - $11,999
  14        $12,000   - $12,999
  15        $13,000   - $13,999
  16        $14,000   - $14,999
  17        $15,000 or Over

Thank you very much; we certainly appreciate your cooperation.

76   60.   (INTERVIEWER: Rate the respondent's house from outside
and inside appearance to you, and from general furni-
ture according to the following categories:)

   1   Adequate (House painted inside and out, porches
and steps are in good condition; walls, couch,
and doors are rather new, or in very good condition)

   2   Medium (Old paint on outside and inside; un-
painted porches and steps, odd pieces of furni-
ture, unclean or "cluttered" walls)

   3   Inadequate (Dilapidated and anything less than
medium)

<u>CODE KEY FOR UNCODED QUESTIONS</u>

<u>CARD #1</u>

<u>IBM Cols. 11, 12 Q. 6.a.</u>

00   Not Applicable (Unemployed, Retired, Student, Military, Housewife, Invalid)

PROFESSIONAL, TECHNICAL, AND MANAGERIAL OCCUPATIONS

01   Occupations in architecture and engineering
02   Occupations in mathematics and physical sciences
04   Occupations in life sciences
05   Occupations in social sciences
07   Occupations in medicine and health
09   Occupations in education
10   Occupations in museum, library, and archival sciences
11   Occupations in law and jurisprudence
12   Occupations in religion and theology
13   Occupations in writing
14   Occupations in art
15   Occupations in entertainment and recreation
16   Occupations in administrative specializations
18   Managers and officials, n.e.c.
19   Miscellaneous professional, technical, and managerial occupations

CLERICAL AND SALES OCCUPATIONS

20   Stenography, typing, filing, and related occupations
21   Computing and account-recording occupations
22   Material and production recording occupations
23   Information and message distribution occupations
24   Miscellaneous clerical occupations
25   Salesmen, services
27   Salesmen and salespersons, commodities
29   Merchandising occupations, except salesmen

118

SERVICE OCCUPATIONS

30   Domestic service occupations
31   Food and beverage preparation and service occupations
32   Lodging and related service occupations
33   Barbering, cosmetology, and related service occupations
34   Amusement and recreation service occupations
35   Miscellaneous personnel service occupations
36   Apparel and furnishings service occupations
37   Protective service occupations
38   Building and related service occupations

FARMING, FISHERY, FORESTRY, AND RELATED OCCUPATIONS

40   Plant farming occupations
41   Animal farming occupations
42   Miscellaneous farming and related occupations
43   Fishery and related occupations
44   Forestry occupations
45   Hunting, trapping, and related occupations
46   Agricultural service occupations

PROCESSING OCCUPATIONS

50   Occupations in processing of metal
51   Ore refining and foundry occupations
52   Occupations in processing of food, tobacco, and related products
53   Occupations in processing of paper and related materials
54   Occupations in processing of petroleum, coal, natural and manufactured gas, and related products
55   Occupations in processing of chemicals, plastics, synthetics, rubber, paint, and related products
56   Occupations in processing of wood and wood products
57   Occupations in processing of stone, clay, glass, and related products
58   Occupations in processing of leather, textiles, and related products
59   Processing occupations, n.e.c.

MACHINE TRADES OCCUPATIONS

60   Metal machining occupations
61   Metal-working occupations, n.e.c.
62
63   Mechanics and machinery repairmen
64   Paperworking occupations
65   Printing occupations
66   Wood machining occupations
67   Occupations in machining stone, clay, glass, and related materials
68   Textiles occupations
69   Machine trades occupations, n.e.c.

BENCH WORK OCCUPATIONS

70   Occupations in fabrication, assembly, and repair of metal products, n.e.c.
71   Occupations in fabrication and repair of scientific and medical apparatus, photographic and optical goods, watches and clocks, and related products
72   Occupations in assembly and repair of electrical equipment
73   Occupations in fabrication and repair of products made from assorted materials
74   Painting, decorating, and related occupations
75   Occupations in fabrication and repair of plastics, synthetics, rubber, and related products
76   Occupations in fabrication and repair of wood products
77   Occupations in fabrication and repair of sand, stone, clay, and glass products
78   Occupations in fabrication and repair of textile, leather, and related products
79   Bench work occupations, n.e.c.

STRUCTURAL WORK OCCUPATIONS

80   Occupations in metal fabricating, n.e.c.
81   Welders, flame cutters, and related occupations
82   Electrical assembling, installing, and repairing occupations
84   Painting, plastering, waterproofing, cementing, and related occupations
85   Excavating, grading, paving, and related occupations
86   Construction occupations, n.e.c.
89   Structural work occupations, n.e.c.

MISCELLANEOUS OCCUPATIONS

90	Motor freight occupations
91	Transportation occupations, n.e.c.
92	Packaging and materials handling occupations
93	Occupations in extraction of minerals
94	Occupations in logging
95	Occupations in production and distribution of utilities
96	Amusement, recreation, and motion picture occupations, n.e.c.
97	Occupations in graphic art work
99	No answer

IBM Col. 13 Q. 6.b.

0	Not Applicable (Full or part-time employed, retired, student, military, housewife)
1	Sick, disabled
2	Can't find a job
3	Others
9	No or Irrelevant answer

IBM Col. 38 Q. 19.a.

0	Not Applicable (Don't know, it depends, and yes answers to Q. 19)
1	General satisfaction with and likeness of place around here
2	Likes doctors and hospitals around here
3	Likes teachers and schools around here
4	Likes home and neighborhood
5	Likes acquaintances, relatives, friends, and social activities
6	Likes my job
7	Likes climate and weather
8	Others
9	No or Irrelevant answer

IBM Col. 40 Q. 19.b.

0	Not Applicable (No or yes answers to Q. 19)
7	Kind of job
8	Others
9	No or Irrelevant answer

IBM Col. 41 Q. 19.c.

0	Not Applicable (No or don't know answers to Q. 19)
1	General dissatisfaction with place around here
2	Dissatisfied with doctors and hospitals around here
3	Dissatisfied with teachers and schools around here
4	Dissatisfied with home and neighborhood
5	Dissatisfied with acquaintances, relatives, friends, and social activities around here
6	Dissatisfied with my job
7	Dissatisfied with the climate and weather around here
8	Others
9	No or Irrelevant answers

IBM Col. 42 Q. 19.c.2.

0	Not Applicable (No or don't know answers to Q. 19)
1	Couldn't afford it
2	Family didn't agree
3	Couldn't find a job
4	Couldn't find a house
5	Own my home
8	Others
9	No or Irrelevant answer

IBM Col. 46 Q. 41

0	Not Applicable (Retired, Invalid)
1	Professional, technical, and managerial occupations
2	Clerical and sales occupations
3	Service occupations
4	Farming, fishery, forestry, and related occupations
5	Processing occupations
6	Machines trades occupations
7	Bench work occupations
8	Structural work occupations
9	Miscellaneous occupations

IBM Col. 48 Q. 42

0	Not Applicable (Retired, Invalid, or No answers)
1	Professional, technical, and managerial occupations
2	Clerical and sales occupations
3	Service occupations

IBM Col. 48 Q. 42 (cont'd)

4	Farming, fishery, forestry, and related occupations
5	Processing occupations
6	Machines trades occupations
7	Bench work occupations
8	Structural work occupations
9	Miscellaneous occupations

IBM Col. 50 Q. 43

0	No or Irrelevant answer
1	Do nothing
2	Watch TV or radio
3	Work around house, garden, etc.
4	Walk or drive around
5	Read
6	Fishing, hunting
7	Sewing, quilting, etc.
9	Others

IBM Col. 51 Q. 44

0	No or Irrelevant answer
1	Like doctors and hospitals around here
2	Like teachers and schools around here
3	Like home and neighborhood
4	Like acquaintances, relatives, friends and social activities
5	Like my job
6	Like climate and weather
7	General likeness
8	Familiarity with place
9	Others

IBM Col. 52 Q. 45

0	No or Irrelevant answer
1	Dislike doctors and hospitals
2	Dislike teachers and schools
3	Dislike home and neighborhood
4	Dislike acquaintances, relatives, friends, and social activities
5	No jobs
6	Dislike climate and weather
7	General dislikes
8	Distance from other service centers, roads
9	Others

IBM Col. 53 Q. 46

0	No or Irrelevant answer
1	Better doctors and hospitals
2	Better teachers and schools
3	Better home and neighborhood
4	Better acquaintances, friends, and social activities
5	Better jobs
6	Better weather and climate
7	Roads, better transportation
8	General improvement
9	Others

IBM Col. 54 Q. 47

0	No or Irrelevant answer
1	Improve water supply and house
2	Pay debts
3	Buy car, TV
4	Save it
5	Personal items
6	Buy land
9	Others

CARD #3

IBM Col. #	Code	Items and Instructions
1	3	Card #3
2,3,4		Schedule Number (With Col. #2 indicating the code number for Postal Route on Col. 5)
5		Postal Routes
	1	La Follette
	2	Duff
	3	Morley
	4	Caryville and Pioneer
	6	Elk Valley
	7	Clairfield and Eagan
7,8		Migration Index (Sum Total of Cols. 36, 37, 45 and 46 of Card #1)

IBM Col. #	Code	Items and Instructions
11,12		General Satisfaction Index (Sum Totals of Cols. 5 and 19 of Card #2)
15,16		Satisfaction with Job Index (Sum Total of Cols. 6, 7, 20 and 21 of Card #2)
19,20		Satisfaction with Health Index (Sum Total of Cols. 8, 9, 22, 23 of Card #2)
23,24		Satisfaction with Education Index (Sum Total of Cols. 10, 11, 24 and 25 of Card #2)
27,28		Satisfaction with House Index (Sum Total of Cols. 12, 13, 14, 26 and 27 of Card #2)
31,32		Satisfaction with Family and Community Ties Index (Sum Total of Cols. 15, 16, 17, 28, 29 and 30 of Card #2)
35,36		Satisfaction with Weather and Climate Index (Sum Total of Cols. 18 and 31 of Card #2)
(41-52)		Number of Family Members, excluding husband and wife according to following age categories (Code actual number; Code 9 for 9 or more members):
41		1 - 4 Years
42		5 - 9 Years
43		10 -14 Years
44		15 19 Years
45		20 -24 Years
46		25 -29 Years
47		30 -34 Years
48		35 -44 Years
49		45 -54 Years
50		55 -64 Years
51		65 -74 Years
52		75 and over

BIBLIOGRAPHY

Books

Alchian, Armen A., and William R. Allen. University Economics. 2nd ed. Belmont, California: Wadsworth Publishing Company, Inc., 1967.

Blalock, Hubert M. Causal Inferences in Nonexperimental Research. Chapel Hill, North Carolina: The University of North Carolina Press, 1964.

Bogue, Donald J. "International Migration," The Study of Population. ed. Philip Hauser and Otis Dudley Duncan. Chicago: University of Chicago Press, 1959.

"International Migration and National Origins of the Population," The Population of the United States. Glencoe, Ill.: The Free Press, 1959. pp. 348-74.

Brunner, Edmund de S. The Growth of a Science: A Half Century of Rural Sociological Research in the U.S. New York: Harper, 1957.

Duncan, Otis Dudley and Albert J. Reiss, Jr. Social Characteristics of Urban and Rural Communities, 1950. New York: Wiley Press, 1950.

Duncan, Otis Durant. "The Theory and Consequences of Mobility of Farm Population," Population Theory and Policy. Ed., Joseph J. Spengler and Otis Dudley Duncan. Glencoe, Ill.: The Free Press, 1956. pp. 417-34.

Francis, Roy G. "Some Elementary Logic," An Introduction to Social Research. 2nd ed. ed. John T. Doley. New York: Appleton-Century-Crofts, 1967.

Goode, William J., and Paul K. Hatt. Methods in Social Research. New York: McGraw-Hill Book Company, Inc., 1952.

Goodrich, Carter, and Others. Migration and Economic Opportunities. Philadelphia: University of Pennsylvania Press, 1936.

Hamilton, C. Horace. "Population Pressure and Other Factors Affecting Net Rural-Urban Migration," Population Theory and Policy. Eds. Joseph J. Spengler and Otis Dudley Duncan, Glencoe, Ill.: The Free Press, 1956. pp. 419-24.

Hauser, Philip M. "Present Status and Prospects of Research in Population," Population Theory and Policy. Eds. Joseph J. Spengler and Otis Dudley Duncan. Glencoe, Ill.: The Free Press, 1956. pp. 70-85.

Kant, Edgar. "Classification and Problems of Migrations," Readings in Cultural Geography. Ed. Philip L. Wagner and Marvin W. Mikesell. Chicago: University of Chicago Press, 1962. pp. 342-54.

Kerlinger, Fred N. Foundations of Behavioral Research: Educational and Psychological Inquiry. New York: Holt, Rinehart and Winston, Inc., 1964.

Lansing, John B., and Eva Mueller. The Geographic Mobility of Labor. Ann Arbor, Michigan: Institute for Social Research, The University of Michigan, 1967.

Lazarsfeld, Paul F., and Morris Rosenberg. The Language of Social Research. Glencoe, Ill.: The Free Press of Glencoe, 1955.

Mangalam, J. J. Human Migration. Lexington, Kentucky: University of Kentucky Press, 1968.

McNemar, Quinn. Psychological Statistics. 3rd ed. New York: John Wiley and Sons, Inc., 1962.

Petersen, William. Population. New York: The Macmillan Company, 1961.

Runciman, W. G. Relative Deprivation and Social Justice: A Study of Attitudes to Social Inequality in Twentieth-Century England. Berkeley, California: University of California Press, 1966.

Seltiz, Claire, and Others. Research Methods in Social Relations. Washington, D.C.: Holt, Rinehart and Winston, Inc., 1963.

Siegel, Sidney. Nonparametric Statistics for the Behavioral Sciences. New York: McGraw-Hill Book Company, Inc., 1956.

Sorokin, A., and Carle C. Zimmerman. Principles of Rural-Urban Sociology. New York: Holt, 1929.

Stouffer, Samuel A. and Others. The American Soldier, I: Adjustment During Army Life. Princeton: C. 1949.

Vance, Rupert B. "Is Theory for Demographers?" Population Theory and Policy. Eds. Joseph J. Spengler and Otis Dudley Duncan. Glencoe, Ill.: The Free Press, 1956. pp. 88-94.

Articles and Periodicals

Anderson, Theodore R. "Intermetropolitan Migration: A Correlation Analysis." The American Journal of Sociology, LXI (March, 1956), 459-62.

Brown, James S., and Others. "Kentucky Mountain Migration and the Stem-Family: An American Variation on a Theme by LePlay." Rural Sociology, XXVIII (March, 1963), 48-69.

Folger, J. K. "Some Aspects of Migration in the Tennessee Valley." American Sociological Review, XVIII (C., 1953), 253-60.

Fuiguit, Glenn V. "Part-Time Farming and the Push-Pull Hypothesis." The American Journal of Sociology, LXIV (January, 1959), 375-379.

Heberle, Rudolf. "Types of Migration." Southwestern Social Science Quarterly, XXXVI (June, 1955), 65-70.

Hillery, George A., and Others. "Migration Systems of the Southern Appalachians: Some Demographic Observations." Rural Sociology, XXX (March, 1965), 33-48.

Lee, Everett S. "A Theory of Migration." Demography, III (C., 1966), 47-57.

Mangalam, J. J., and Harry K. Schwarzweller. "General Theory in the Study of Migration: Current Needs and Difficulties." The International Migration Review, III (Fall, 1968), 3-18.

McGinnis, Robert. "Randomization and Inference in Sociological Research." American Sociological Review, XXII (October, 1957), 411.

Ravenstein, E. G. "The Laws of Migration." Journal of the Royal Statistical Society, XLVIII, Part 2 (June, 1885), 167-227.

"The Laws of Migration." Journal of the Royal Statistical Society, LII (June, 1889), 241-301.

Schwarzweller, Harry K., and James S. Brown. "Social Class Origins, Rural Urban Migration, and Economic Life Changes: A Case Study." Rural Sociology, XXXII (March, 1967), 5-19.

Senior, Clarence. "Migration as a Process and Migrant as a Person." Population Review, VI (January, 1962), 30-41.

Stouffer, Samuel A. "Intervening Opportunities: A Theory Relating Mobility and Distance." American Sociological Review, V (December, 1940), 845-67.

"Intervening Opportunities and Competing Migrants." Journal of Regional Science, XI (C., 1960), 1-26.

Tarver, James D. "Predicting Migration." Social Forces, XXXIX (March, 1961), 207-14.

Zipf, George K. "The P_1P_2/D Hypothesis: On the Intercity Movement of Persons." American Sociological Review, XI (December, 1946), 677-86.

Unpublished Materials

Brennan, Michael J. "Regional Labor and Capital Migration." Unpublished Report, Contract No. C-325-65. Providence, Rhode Island. Brown University, 1967.

Doerflinger, Jon Arno. "Patterns of Internal Migration Related to Institutional and Age-Sex Structure of the U.S." Unpublished doctoral dissertation. University of Wisconsin, 1962. Dissertation Abstracts, XXIII. December-January, 1962-1963. p.2238.

East Tennessee Development District. "Campbell County Demonstration Project: A Comprehensive Plan." Unpublished Report. East Tennessee Development District. Knoxville, Tennessee, 1969.

Johnson, Ronald L., and James J. Kiefert. "Factors Involved in the Decision to Migrate and the Impact of Migration Upon the Individual and the Sender and Receiver Community." Unpublished Report, Project No. 6-1663 for the U.S. Department of Health, Education and Welfare. Grand Forks, North Dakota, University of North Dakota, 1968.

Others

Bogue, Donald J., and Others. "Subregional Migration in the United States, 1935-1940." Vol. I. Streams of Migration. Oxford, Ohio: Scripps Foundation Studies in Population Distribution, No. 5, 1957.

Brown, James S., and George A. Hillery, Jr. "The Great Migration, 1940-1960." <u>The Southern Appalachian Region: A Survey</u>. Ed. Thomas R. Ford. Lexington: University of Kentucky Press, 1962. pp. 54-78.

Folger, John K. "Models in Migration." <u>Selected Studies of Migration Since World War II, Proceedings of the 34th Annual Conference of the Milbank Memorial Fund</u>, Part III. New York: 1957. pp. 155-64.

Hofstee, E. W. "Some Remarks on Selective Migration." <u>Research Group for European Migration Problems</u>, Publication 7. The Hague: Nijhoff, 1952.

Schwarzweller, Harry K. <u>Family Ties, Migration, and Transitional Adjustment of Young Men from Eastern Kentucky</u>. University of Kentucky Agricultural Experiment Station, Bulletin 691, Lexington, Kentucky: University of Kentucky, 1964.

Thomas, Dorothy S. "Age and Economic Differentials in Internal Migration in the United States: Structure and Distance." <u>International Population Conference</u>. Vienna: Union Internationale Pour l'Etude Scientifique de la Population, 1959. pp. 714-721.

BIOGRAPHICAL SKETCH

The author was born in Jebrail, Lebanon on December 15, 1934. He was educated in public primary schools in Lebanon, and in secondary schools in Lebanon and Switzerland, receiving a diploma in agriculture from Ecole Cantonale d'Agriculture, Cernier, Neuchatel, Switzerland in 1953. Upon his graduation from Switzerland, he taught at Jebrail Rural Fellowship Center, Lebanon, from 1953 to 1956.

In 1956 the author left Lebanon to attend Montana State College, University of Tennessee, and Ohio State University, receiving from the latter a Bachelor of Science in Rural Sociology. Following his graduation from Ohio State University, he worked as the director of the Akkar Area - Cooperative and Training Program in Lebanon from 1960 to 1964. In 1964 the author left Lebanon again to attend Michigan State University, receiving a Master of Arts in Communications and a minor in Sociology in 1965. He left to Lexington in 1965 to spend three years in residence at the University of Kentucky in pursuit of a Doctor of Philosophy in Sociology with a minor in Economics. In 1967 he was married to the former Roswitha Hausser of Ludwigshafen, Germany. In 1968 the author became the director of Campbell County Demonstration Project of the East Tennessee Development District. In 1970 the author returned to the University of Kentucky to work as a teaching assistant and lecturer at the Department of Sociology while completing his dissertation.

ATTITUDE TOWARDS MIGRATION AMONG RURAL RESIDENTS: STAGES AND FACTORS INVOLVED IN THE DECISION TO MIGRATE

BY: SAMIR N.MAAMARY